CONTENTS

Chapter 1
The saga of Stumpy   3

Chapter 2
An Appledore mariner's last voyage   12

Chapter 3
Appledore vessels   21

Chapter 4
Some Appledore sayings   32

Chapter 5
Fishing the Taw and Torridge estuary   50

Chapter 6
Appledore cooking   69

Afterword   83

Foreword

Memories of an Appledore 'maid'

When we wrote our last book, Appledore Rope Mats and Memories of an Appledore Maid, we wanted to include an insight into the lifestyles of the inhabitants of this maritime village from the beginning of the twentieth century, which was about the time our parents were born. The changes that both they and our generation saw mostly took place after the Second World War. As a consequence, some of these insights into local life inevitably began to creep into the book, so it was suggested to us that we should include just some 'snippets' of these in the book so as to turn what could have been an instruction book on how to construct different types of rope mats in the traditional Appledore style, into something that also gave some idea of what life was like in Appledore before it became the place it is today. The other stories I'd collected which were part of the social history of Appledore would be enlarged upon in a later volume. And here it is.

Since the Second World War great changes have taken place in the village but, because Appledore was almost a 'closed' community with little influence coming from the outside, changes, when they did come, came thick and fast. My father could remember the ladies who picked laver in the winter months without shoes on their feet, although I personally cannot remember this, along with other things from my childhood which have also been lost – sometimes this is for the good, but sometimes there are things that we locals are not so sure ought to have been lost.

By the time I was three months old it was the end of June and the summer season for bass fishing had begun. The year being 1944, the war was still being fought, so there were still some restrictions on what the population could or could not do. But fishing was not one of them. I was taken out with my parents in their 14-foot clinker-built boat which was powered by paddles (either my mother or father rowing) or by a small lug sail. As a cheel (child) I was either laid in a wooden box or, if the lug sail was not set, i.e. they were fishing at anchor, a fold would be made in the sail (hammock style) and I would be laid in it. This early introduction to the sea resulted in a strong interest in the natural world around me and learning the skills of anything connected with the sea as I grew up.

By the age of ten I was given my own 10-foot clinker-built punt (dinghy) and left to my own devices, making fishing lines and picking crabs to be used as bait. There were only two rules: firstly, not to go 'out along' (out of the estuary towards the bar); and the second was not to take anyone with me – my father did not want the responsibility of someone else's cheel drowning. Obviously there was no safety gear in the form of life preservers, nor were there any flares, mainly because they were considered not to be needed, as the cheel was brought up to respect the river and sea. And the river traffic in those days was almost nil: a few hardy souls would occasionally come to Instow for a water skiing holiday, but they would confine themselves to the designated ski area which was Crow Point at the mouth of the River Taw.

In this small volume we have touched on just some of the stories and lives of the characters who have lived in the village. There are, I'm sure, many, many more. Almost every family who has lived in the village for generations will almost certainly have some of their own yarns to tell which would give other insights into the life and times of the indigenous residents of Appledore.

Ann Wells 2013

CHAPTER 1

The saga of Stumpy

■ Introduction

The tinsel town of Hollywood has had in its history animal stars that have been loved by generations of children and adults alike. The two wonder dogs, Lassie and Rin Tin Tin, the wonder horse Champion, Flipper the dolphin and, of course, from the Antipodes, Skippy the kangaroo who with great agility would bounce across our television screens and enthral us all those years ago. All these creatures entertained us with unbelievable feats of almost human ingenuity, but always emerging unscathed and ready to do or die again in the next episode. Stumpy, on the other hand, was not a star – but was destined to become one and to become a much loved character in the village.

■ The arrival of Stumpy

Stumpy was a young herring gull (*Larus argentatus*) about a year old and still sporting his juvenile plumage when he arrived on the roof of a shed in the back yard of a cottage in Irsha street, Appledore, on the 1st of June 1997. Both his legs had been entangled in monofilament fishing line, which had tightened, resulting in both his legs withering and dropping off, one below the knee joint and the other through the knee joint. This would have been a long and painful process for the bird, so when the exhausted and weakened bird landed on the shed roof the owner was able to catch the gull and remove the remaining line and clean the wounds: thus began the saga of Stumpy.

Life for this gull without webbed feet was very difficult indeed but flying freely was not, nor was landing and taking off from water too much of a problem, it was the landing and taking off from the hard beach or the shed roof that was difficult for him, but he was able to adapt and became quite skilled in his landings.

Luckily for Stumpy the owner of the shed was a fisherman called Roy who was sympathetic towards the bird. Stumpy very quickly learnt that this was a good berth, where food was readily available for him alone as the man stood guard over the dish of food keeping other gulls away. So Stumpy adopted Roy and trained him to provide tasty morsels such as tins of cat food – salmon and tuna flavoured, of course! – getting through at least six tins a week. He also enjoyed the remains of the Sunday joint and when Roy had been fishing and caught a few fish he also feasted on the livers from the fish. Very soon on this exclusive diet Stumpy began to recover from his injuries. But this fine living did not seem to satisfy Stumpy, because he would also visit Roy's neighbours and they would provide bread and cakes.

Stumpy on the shed roof in Appledore

All in all Stumpy had found himself a good berth and in consequence was as fit and well as any herring gull could expect to be.

■ Tracks and sprats

When the tide had ebbed sufficiently Roy would go down to the beach to inspect his boat and pump out any rainwater which had accumulated in her and check that the moorings were secure. Roy would notice that Stumpy was around because he could see the tracks of his stumps across the sand ridge by the two holes made in the soft sand. During the summer months Stumpy would make excursions across the estuary at low tide to an area known as Crow Pits. These are large and sometimes deep pools – perhaps up to two foot deep – which are made in the sand by the swirling eddies of the ebb tide. Small fish such as white-bait (known locally as brit) and sand eels would become trapped in these pools and Stumpy, along with his other gull friends would hunt for them. Stumpy propelled himself across the water with his stumps with great alacrity, and ducking his head deep down into the water he would catch his share of these tasty morsels. His stumps must have been turbo charged! But even after a good day over in the Pits he would always return to his berth on the shed roof in Irsha Street when the tide came in or when it became 'dimpsy' (twilight) after spending an enjoyable day fishing. But he would still be hungry enough to eat any handouts that Roy would put out for him.

During one particularly hot and humid summer, Stumpy became infested with parasites. It is not unusual for birds to have a resident population of lice and bird fleas, but for a bird without the means of scratching with claws to dislodge these creatures from the body it must have been pretty uncomfortable. The lice and fleas must have known that they were going to be safe around the neck of Stumpy because that is where they congregated, causing the feathers to drop out and the skin to become raw. Roy was most concerned for the well-being of Stumpy, but as a wild bird it would have been difficult to catch him so that treatment for the condition could be given. However, when the autumn rains came it gently washed the infected areas on his neck and after a few weeks there was a marked improvement in the condition. The clean rainwater, which was slightly acidic, acted as an antiseptic and gently cleaned the wounds. During the following winter months, with the aid of a good diet ,the feathers on Stumpy's neck grew back as good as new.

■ Flying incident

Stumpy had several flight paths to choose from, but it depended on the wind direction which one he chose when landing on the shed roof. One day Stumpy had an unfortunate accident. It was feeding time and Roy had gone out into the yard to place the food in the usual place on the roof of the shed. Roy saw Stumpy coming in (like aircraft, birds land and take off into the wind); this particular day the wind was such that he had taken the 'ducks alley' flight path when he just dropped out of the sky. Roy was both mystified and concerned as there was no apparent reason why this should have happened. Roy went to the back wall, which is also the sea wall, just in time to see Stumpy coming up again. Poor old Stumpy was caught up and was bouncing up and down on a fishing line which Roy's neighbour had cast out over his back wall! Roy asked his neighbour not to reel in the line because of the danger of Stumpy getting hooked, and began to put the ladder out over the wall in an attempt to free the unfortunate gull. But luckily before Roy had manoeuvred the ladder out over the wall Stumpy was able to free himself without any apparent physical injury, but was obviously shaken by the ordeal.

■ Christmas fare

Christmas was fast approaching and for some time Roy had been busy catching and preparing the ingredients for a succulent Christmas surprise for Stumpy. Some of his favourite morsels had been gathered and made into a very tasty Christmas pudding. Sand eels (sprats), crabs' legs in aspic, cockles, mussels, limpets, and boiled cod's heads were all mixed together with Stumpy's favourite, a can of salmon and tuna cat food. All these ingredients had been bound together with a very rich seafood sauce liberally laced with cod liver oil, then placed into a basin and pressed down with a saucer with a weight on it and chilled in the fridge. All this had been done as a surprise Christmas Day lunch, but since the incident with the fishing line Stumpy was unwilling to come in and feed on the roof of Roy's shed. That incident must have reminded him of the time when he became entangled in the discarded monofilament line which resulted in him losing both his legs. Roy was concerned about this and was considering taking the pudding down on the beach where Stumpy could land in safety and enjoy his festive fare, but as things turned out Stumpy regained his confidence and returned to having his meals on the roof of Roy's shed well before the big day. As Roy stood guard to prevent any interlopers diving in to steal any of the fare Stumpy tucked into the meal and then settled down on the roof, put his head under his wing and went to sleep. Having seen all was well, Roy went back into his kitchen and tucked into his own Christmas lunch, then after washing the dishes and tidying up sat in his armchair and nodded off to sleep himself.

■ Peeping Toms

When Roy decided that he would have a bathroom make-over, little did he know what trouble he would have with his feathered neighbours when the nesting season began. All went well with this operation: the new suite was ordered, delivered and duly installed, the walls tiled, and new cabinets and cupboards built. But as Roy was doing the work himself (an Appledore man by trade!) this exercise had taken a few months, and in the meantime a pair of herring gulls had chosen the flat roof of his next door neighbour as a possible nest site. Stumpy did not seem to mind this as long as they did not intrude on his patch or try to steal any of his grub. For Roy, however, it was a different story altogether because this pair of herring gulls would stand on the window sill of the bathroom, peer in and watch with great interest the action going on inside. Of course, this might have been an innocent manoeuvre on their part – they might just have been looking at their reflections in the glass – but Roy felt sure that Stumpy had had a hand in this, because very often Stumpy was to be seen on his shed roof calling as if egging them on!

■ Birthday celebrations

Having been mates for getting on for three and a half years Roy thought it would be fitting to have a party to celebrate the arrival of the gull on the roof of his shed. All this time Stumpy had been living in 'cloud gull-land', with Roy providing good grub and a relatively safe place for him to rest. As Stumpy had arrived on the 1st of June, that was the date Roy chose as the day for the 'party of the year'.

For several days prior to the event, Roy had been busy collecting mussels, limpets, crabs and sand eels, there were also several tins of salmon and tuna flavoured cat food which had been donated by well-wishers. The morning dawned bright and clear like it can in late spring/early summer in this part of the world and Roy was up very early on this first day of June to start the preparations for 'The' birthday party.

Because a large number of guests were expected, two very large plates of salmon and tuna sandwiches were made with stale bread and the filling donated by well-wishers. Stumpy's gull mates loved these, and his friends the pied wagtails, sparrows and starlings who lived in the various nooks, crannies and outhouses of the cottages in Irsha Street could join in, eating the bread and gathering up the crumbs for their babies which were still in the nests, so that they too would be part of the celebration. A pair of pied wagtails Stumpy was particularly fond of had their nest, which contained four young, in the forward locker of a boat down on the beach. The wood around the Samson post had rotted away and the enterprising wagtails had built a nest in the space below where the anchor and rode were housed When the tide was out, the adults would scour the beach for flies and small crustaceans and would not have far to travel, but every six hours the boat would be afloat so the birds would have to fly a greater distance to and from a from the boat to feed their young, so the crumbs from the sandwiches would have been a real bonus for these little birds.

■ The party menu

A great deal of thought had gone into the menu for the party, and the items which had been gathered from the beach were carefully prepared. Many of Stumpy's gull friends enjoyed the delicacy of crabs legs in aspic, so several dishes of this favourite was prepared. Also there were bowls of limpet delight and crab trifle with, of course, a generous drop of medicinal cod liver oil at the base. There were, unfortunately, those who over-imbibed this mixture and in consequence were sick as gulls for their efforts. The birthday cake was the *pièce de résistance*. Roy had put his extensive culinary knowledge to work into making this magnificent creation: of course, there were one or two secret ingredients, but the main ingredients were mussels and cockles. These had been cooked to perfection and drained, placed in a basin, and pressed down and chilled in the refrigerator for several hours. When it was time to present the cake to Stumpy it was turned out on to a large tray and three very large and succulent sand eels were stuck into the cake, head uppermost: and as only one breath is allowed to blow out the candles on a birthday cake, it is also the tradition with gulls that all the sand eels on the cake should be consumed in one gulp. Stumpy did this with great verve and panache and was able to make his wish. The cake was then shared out amongst his gully friends.

■ The end of a perfect day

That evening Peter and Joan sat in the bus shelter opposite the Seagate Hotel with George, Joan's father. George had noticed a lone seagull sitting on the railing and told Joan that during that afternoon there were hundreds along there. Joan told her father it had been Stumpy's birthday party, and what he had seen was the guests going home with a bag of goodies and a balloon, and this particular gull might have over-indulged in the richness of the party food and was not feeling too well. A lady visitor who had been sitting at the other end of the bench got up, gathered herself together and quickly walked away, shaking her head. Stumpy, on the other hand, sat on the shed roof, shook his head and tail a couple of times, put his head under his wing, and dozed off to sleep a very happy gull.

■ Celebrity status and end piece

Over the years Roy and Stumpy became very well known in the village. People would stop and inquire of Roy how Stumpy was getting on. And from time to time presents of tins of salmon and tuna cat food would be left on the door-step of Roy's cottage by well-wishers. Regular news updates of the exploits of Stumpy were printed in the Parish Magazine, and through the magazine Roy would pass on messages of thanks from Stumpy for the food parcels and the good wishes from his many fans. And for several years St. Mary's Church was illuminated in celebration of his birthday on June 1st.

Stumpy paddling in the river

Sadly, in 2002, Roy died and Stumpy was left on his own. Roy had a brother who from time to time would visit Roy's now empty cottage to make sure everything was in order. But because he didn't live in the village he couldn't carry on looking after Stumpy as Roy had done, so after a while Stumpy disappeared and no one saw him on the beach or on any of the flat roof tops along Irsha Street. He had just vanished. But between them, he and Roy had left stories and memories that will be remembered in Appledore for many years to come.

Everything you ever wanted to know about Herring Gulls...

Herring Gull (*Larus argentatus*)

- Resident breeding bird and winter visitor.
- Lives on coasts, lakes and rivers.
- Most familiar of the seaside seagulls.
- Eats mostly animal food, but also scavenges and will rob other birds of their food: will also rob children of ice cream and adults of chips!
- Has been seen using bread as bait to catch goldfish.
- They are 'worm charmers'. They drum their feet on the ground (called 'paddling') to bring earthworms to the surface.
- Their feet are tough and leathery, enabling them to perch on spikes and sharp objects.
- First began nesting on roofs in the south-west of England in the 1920s.
- Will attack if they think their nest is threatened.
- Has one brood per year and usually lays three eggs: won't breed until at least 4 years old.
- There are around 130,000 herring gulls in the UK: about 12% of the world population.
- Their numbers have declined substantially in recent years and they are now on 'The RED List'.

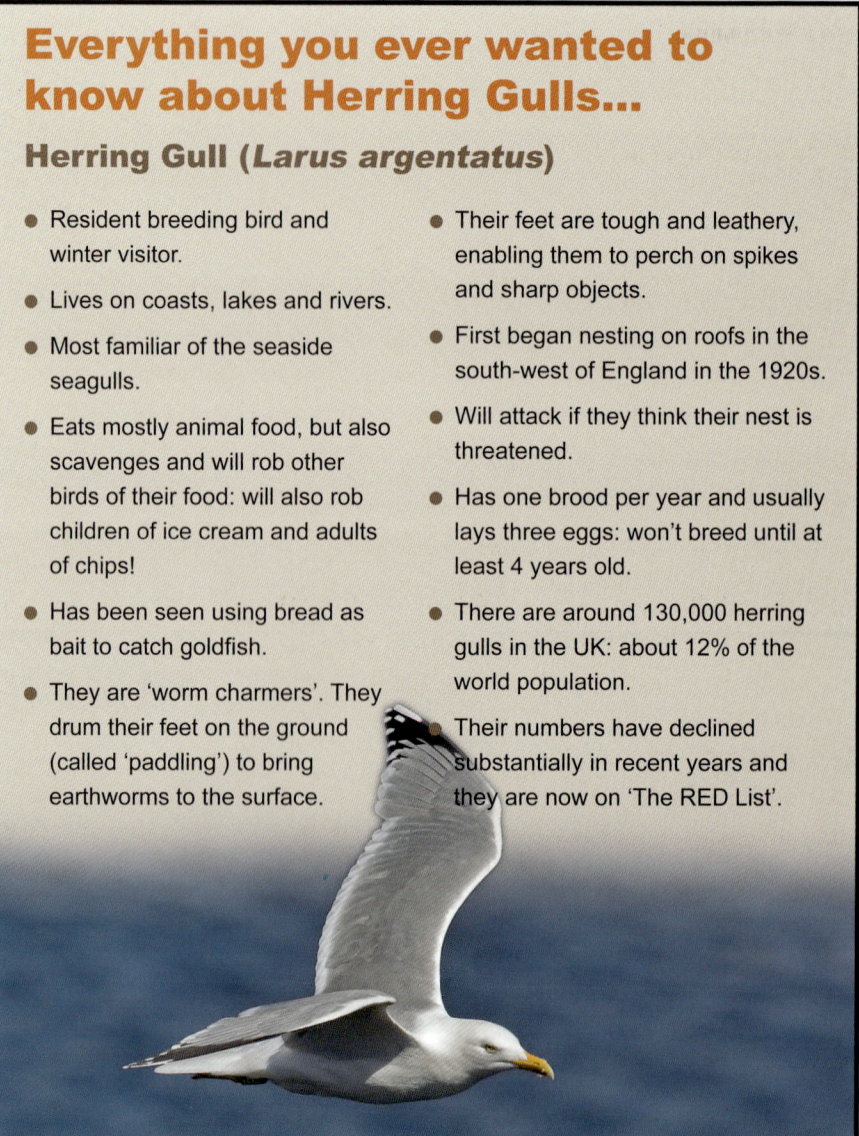

Chapter 2

An Appledore mariner's last voyage

■ *Master Mariners*

The north coast of Devon and Cornwall is notorious for its rugged cliffs and rocky shoals, huge Atlantic swells, wild storms, hazardous harbour entrances and shipwrecks. Although this account does not involve a shipwreck it illustrates that the seamen in the years before the Second World War knew how to cope single-handedly with the unforeseen. These seafarers sailed the world's oceans in the large sailing ships of that era, and it was not until later in their years at sea did they experience engines or even basic radio communications.

For centuries, the mariners from Appledore were known the world over for their outstanding skills in seamanship. From their courage and bravery against the Spanish Armada in 1588, when Appledore was granted free port status, to the shipbuilding industry that supplied the boats for the American colonists and the fishing and cargo ships in the era of ocean-going sail, Appledore has been a significant player in England's maritime history. Many of these men were Master Mariners and often they would take on the captaincy of small coastal sailing vessels, thus only being away from home for short periods. Trading as they did from port to port in and around the Bristol Channel, the Isle of Man, Ireland (north and south), the Isles of Scilly and around the coast to ports in south Devon and Cornwall, these sailing vessels were what the great juggernauts of today are on our roads. And many of these seafaring men also sailed as crew aboard the great J-Class yachts during the fiercely competitive yacht-racing seasons of the 1920s and early 1930s. This is a story about two of those brave and enterprising Appledorian seamen.

Today breaking news flies across the globe as soon as there is some man-made or natural disaster or a piece of gripping news occurs. No one is out of reach of the media anywhere for very long. Indeed, with the technology of mobile phones which are able to take photographs, and with the facility to be able to send them through the ether via the internet to a news station, we are all now able to see incidents happening live. Imagine then, being in a situation where you are at sea, sailing past the north Devon and Cornwall coast with a mate. It is your off-watch period so you go down below to rest. Then you awake, because the movement of the vessel is not right and go on deck to find that your mate is dead at the tiller. There is no communications equipment except for flags to use as signals, which had to be bent on and hoisted up the mast to be read by any passing ship or coastguard watch station. The following account is of just such a tragedy. The death, inquest and funeral of Captain White, an ill-fated mariner, is pieced together from reports of the time by unknown newspapers, family recollections and photographs of the two mariners involved.

■ The start of a pleasant voyage

On Saturday, 26th of May 1934, the pilot cutter rigged yacht *Seafarer* was being taken from Ilfracombe to Salcombe for its owner Dr Russell by Captain John White and Captain Joseph Bennett. Both of these men were highly experienced Master Mariners. The vessel had recently been in the shipyard of P. K. Harris and Sons at Appledore for some reconditioning work to be carried out. Dr Russell, had been aboard the yacht, but because there had been some damage caused to the sails the vessel had to put into Ilfracombe for repairs. Dr Russell was unable to remain whilst the repairs were made so John White took charge of the vessel. The *Seafarer* left Ilfracombe at about six o'clock that evening and everything appeared to be all right. After supper Joseph Bennett went below until about midnight when he returned to the deck to assist the captain. Together they had a hot brew of tea and a smoke, after which John White went below. He relieved Joseph Bennett at the tiller at about 4.00 a.m.

■ Tragedy strikes

About four hours later the unsteady motion of the vessel woke Captain Bennett. The yacht was yawing and off course, and realising that something was amiss and not having had any reply from his shout he went on deck to find Captain White lying in the cockpit. He had been "foaming at the mouth and there was no response to shaking". At that time the yacht was about twenty miles off Trevose Head. He secured the body in the cockpit and turned the yacht around and headed for Padstow some forty or fifty miles away. Heading for shore, and with light coming into the sky, Captain Bennett signalled with flags to the Stepper Point coast guard station near Padstow for a doctor to be at the quayside on arrival.

Arriving at Padstow early in the afternoon Captain Bennett could not enter the harbour until there was sufficient flood tide for the vessel to cross the bar. The entrance to Padstow has a notorious bar, not unlike the one at the mouth of the Taw and Torridge estuary, which can only be crossed when tidal and weather conditions permit. The *Seafarer*'s flag was flying at half-mast and on the quayside to meet this little vessel was Dr Shirvell and police sergeant Mr Climo. Mr White's body was taken to Padstow mortuary.

From Padstow Joseph Bennett telephoned the vicarage at Appledore which was the home port of the two men, and the vicar, the Rev. H. C. A. S. Muller, immediately visited Mrs White and the family to tell them of the devastating news. That evening the Bishop of Crediton, the Right

Reverend William Surtees was the guest preacher at the Evensong service in St. Mary's Parish church and during the service he referred to this tragic event, and the congregation was asked to stand in silent sympathy.

■ The inquest and funeral

On the following day, May 28th, the inquest was held in the Men's Institute at Padstow, which was just a short distance from the harbour where the *Seafarer* was still lying. Mr E. W. Gill, who was the Bodmin and district deputy coroner, recorded that the cause of death was heart failure due to arterial sclerosis (hardening of the arteries): the witnesses were Mr Joseph Frederick Bennett of One End Street, Appledore, a Master Mariner, and Dr E. A. Shirvell of Padstow. The body of Captain White was then returned to Appledore.

The funeral took place at St. Mary's Church, Appledore, on Thursday, May 31st. The sympathy aroused by the tragic death of Captain White filled the church with mourners, including a large number of members of the Royal Antediluvian Order of Buffaloes (RAOB), of which he was a member. The vicar (the Rev. H. C. A. S Muller) officiated at the funeral, and as Provincial Grand Chaplain of the RAOB took some of the RAOB prayers. A Miss Burrington played the organ, and the hymns, *Lead Kindly Light*, *Eternal Father* and *Peace, Perfect Peace* were sung, as well as the ROAB Absent Brethren's hymn, *Spirit of Truth*.

At the graveside, Knight Hinks and Knight Harris led the members of Ye Hubbastone, Ye Amyas Leigh, and Ye Kingsley Lodges in casting the Ivy Leaf into the grave: Amyas Leigh was the principle character of Charles Kingsley's maritime novel, *Westward Ho!*, after which the seaside Victorian village was named, and Hubbastone is the name of the 'rock' in the River Torridge where local people fought off an invasion by Hubba the Dane.

John White: the man

Captain John White was the fourth son of Captain Philip White and was married to Miss Harriet Eastman, eldest daughter of Captain William Eastman and Mrs Eastman. He went to sea as a lad, and after gaining considerable experience in the coasting trade carrying general cargo from port to port, joined the 883-ton iron sailing barque Lutterworth on the UK–Australia and New Zealand run. The Lutterworth was built in 1868 and owned by Messrs Shaw, Savill and Co., and at that time commanded by Captain Richard Kelly, also of Appledore. Captain Kelly died on a voyage in 1900 off New Zealand while in command of the ship Westland. He was just 43 years of age and was carried to his last resting place by the Appledorian crew members on the ship.

After leaving the Lutterworth John White returned to yachting and sailed in some famous yachts. He then commanded various coasting vessels – Express Heatherbell, Maude, Benico, Welsh Belle and Victoria. During the First World War, whilst serving aboard the Lady of the Lake, he was torpedoed and spent several hours at sea in an open boat before being rescued.

Captain White had five daughters and one son. His wife Harriet died on September 23rd 1958 aged 82.

Capt. John White, his wife Harriet, and son John known as 'Jacky'
Photo by kind permission of Mr. Leonard White

■ The other seaman: Captain J. T. Bennett

The other member of the crew of that ill-fated voyage was Joseph Tawton Bennett, also a Master Mariner. He was born on 8th of March 1866 at Irsha Street, Appledore, and was the third son of Captain William Bennett and Elizabeth Bennett, née Tawton. As a boy he sailed with his father on the coastal ketch *Nugget*, and after a few years working the coastal trade and gaining experience went on to what Appledorians called 'deep-water trips'. These deep-water voyages were in barques – sailing vessels having three masts with square rigged sails – and often lasted anything from six months to two years or more. It was on these long voyages when they were off watch or were in the Doldrums that, to relieve the hours of boredom, they turned their hands to traditional sailors' crafts. With an old jack-knife they would carve scrimshaw on to bones, wood and, if available, the tusks of sea mammals. Others perhaps constructed tiny replica ships and put them into bottles. Others made rope mats out of the discarded rope from the rigging or anchor cables. The rope was unlaid into two strands then made into 'foxes' and in turn this was then plaited into 'sennit' (fuller descriptions of rope mat making can be found in the book *Appledore Rope Mats: and memories of a Appledore Maid*).

Life was hard for these mariners and after a few years of deep-water sailing they would come 'ashore' and find employment as a Master Mariner or a first mate on a local vessel to sail in what was known as 'the coastal trade'. Before the Second World War there were a great many schooners and ketches (sailing vessels with two or more masts) in the north Devon and north Cornwall area, which required experienced hands to work them. These experienced seamen were able to reef sails, stand watch, and knew the correct way to load the ship so that the vessel would sail easily. And because they had already gained local experience from the time they had left school and gone on to the coastal trade, they knew the vagaries of the ports and harbours around the coast. These men were also eagerly sought after as crew members by millionaire yacht owners, both because of their vast knowledge of seamanship and their experience. And, like many other Master mariners from Appledore, J. T. Bennett would sign on for the summer sailing season for the likes of Sir Thomas Lipton, the Scottish tea baron who challenged five times for the America's Cup, all in yachts named *Shamrock* to honour his Northern Irish lineage.

■ Man of action

On April 21st 1889 when he was twenty-three years old Joseph Bennett married Elizabeth Ann Johns, the eldest daughter of Mr & Mrs William Johns, a well-known boat-man in the town who became known as 'Daddy' Johns and instigated the Appledore–Instow ferry. Joseph and Elizabeth went on to have ten children: five boys and five girls, with about two years between each child – which was often the length of a deep-water voyage. The first of the children was Alfred, born in 1890, and the last was Verbena, born in 1908.

Capt. J. T. Bennett on the deck of his vessel Mabel with his eldest son Alfred and an unknown crew member

Joseph later took command of the schooner, *Mabel,* and sailed on her in home waters for over twenty years. Often his wife would accompany him, leaving the younger children at home to be cared for by their elder sisters. During those years he had his share of excitement: at one time the *Mabel* was in the company of the ketch *Bonito,* commanded by Captain T. Hutchings, when they were caught in very heavy weather between Holyhead and Liverpool bar. Despite the lifeboat being called, they managed to reach shelter. In 1911 he was shipwrecked in the *Mabel* on Wexford bar, Ireland, and he and his two sons, Alfred and Oswald, were rescued by the Wexford lifeboat.

Joseph Bennett joined as quartermaster on the S.S. *Tainui,* captained at that time by another Appledore man, Alfred Kelly, and served on her during the First World War, mainly on the North Atlantic routes between the UK and Canada, carrying passengers and general cargo. But this was not the last of this mariner's exploits. Because on 27th August 1937, at the age of 72, when he saw a child in difficulty in the River Torridge off Appledore quay, he jumped into the water and saved him: Derrick Curtis was aged 4. For this gallant exploit Joseph was awarded the Royal Humane Society Parchment medal.

Joseph Tawton Bennett and his wife Elizabeth Ann went on to celebrate their Golden Wedding in 1939 with all but one of their children: their son, Wilfred, who had died in 1938. Elizabeth Ann died in 1949 aged 83.

When he died in 1946 Joseph Bennett was one of the last two survivors of the crew of the Appledore lifeboat coxswained by the late William Jenkins which had rescued the crew of the large sailing ship *Penciclea*.

Capt. J T Bennett with Derrick Curtis in the back yard of 18, One End Street, Appledore

Chapter 3

Appledore vessels

■ *Appledore port and mariners*

Appledore was the home of a goodly number of West Country sailing ketches, mostly owned and often captained by Appledorians who were known as Master and Owner. The port of registry would have been Bideford for these vessels, while Braunton vessels would have been registered at the port of Barnstaple. A small number of the Appledore vessels had owners who lived across the estuary at Braunton or upriver from Appledore at Bideford but the captains and crews of these vessels were usually men from Appledore. These experienced men had local knowledge of the tide variants for crossing the bar and were trusted to do their work in a proper seafaring manner; indeed some of these captains of the coastal ketches had sailed the world's great oceans in the square riggers of the day and, in later years, in ships that combined the use of sail and steam.

They were also very familiar with the coastal regions of the Bristol Channel, St. Georges Channel and the tiny ports and harbours around the Cornish coast. From an early age these men had been brought up to handle a small boat, taught how to splice rope and steer a craft, so by the time they left school at the age of fourteen they were proficient seamen. My own father left school one day and sailed out over the bar the next with his father in the ketch *Humility*, a vessel that traded in general cargo until 1920. The length of the oceanic voyages these men embarked on meant that very often they were away from home for up to two years. But Braunton men, too, were very experienced seafarers and worked well with the Appledore men: there would often be a combined crew of both Appledore and Braunton men working alongside each other on the these little coastal vessels. There were usually three men aboard – captain, first mate and a boy, and these three would sail, cook and generally keep the ship in good order whilst on a voyage.

Appledore Quay: with kind permission of the Appledore Historical Society

The West Country sailing vessels themselves were built specifically to trade around the west coast of Britain, but there were times when they ventured east and north away from south west waters, and some of the larger ketches (registered to carry no more than 200 tons) ventured across the Atlantic. These were sturdy little vessels, often registered to carry no more than an average of about 90 tons, and constructed in such a way that when the tide ebbed away from the hull the vessel would remain upright to facilitate easy discharging or loading of the cargo.

Many ports and harbours, especially in the West Country, did not have a proper quay for a vessel to go alongside to discharge or load, so boats were sometimes beached in between a reef of rocks which had to be skilfully negotiated on approach to the beach: these hazardous conditions very often earned a higher than usual freight charge. Horses and carts were driven down to the beach and with the aid of a dolly winch and a spare gaff the crew would empty the hold. This operation did not normally take any longer than two tides: a quick turnaround was imperative to take advantage of calm weather and sea conditions because, if the wind direction changed or a ground swell came up, the vessels would be vulnerable to be being breached or washed up and down the beach, causing damage to the hull. If there was no return cargo then sand from the beach around the vessel would be loaded into the hold to give the ship some ballast. Some smaller ports had stone-built harbours, which allowed vessels to go alongside, so the discharge and loading of cargo was easier there as operations could carry on as the tide ebbed and flowed from the harbour.

Entering and leaving these little harbours was hazardous. An entry could be, perhaps, no more than a small gap between cliffs, where for millions of years a small river or large stream had gouged out a channel between the softer rock formations. The wind in these inlets could come from different directions as it bounced from one cliff face to another – 'flukey', as the sailors called it – making navigation difficult. Boscastle in north Cornwall is one such example. Auxiliary engines reduced the danger, but many of these little ketches did not have auxiliary engines fitted until just before the First World War, and they were often not used unless absolutely necessary as fuel for these engines had to be paid for – but the wind was free!

One of the commonest cargos brought to the Taw/Torridge was limestone. Both rivers had a number of limekilns dotted along their banks, some of which can still be seen today. Lime was spread over ploughed land to, as it was said, 'sweeten the soil'. As a water-soluble substance, natural lime is soon washed out of the soil during the wet winter months, making the land more acid. Adding lime to the soil creates a neutral Ph balance, which makes the land more productive.

Situated along the beach from the Appledore lifeboat house (walking towards Northam Burrows) there was a limekiln which over the years has gradually been eroded away by the sea. Vessels laden with limestone were beached on the shore at the bottom and to the left of the lifeboat slip then, as the tide ebbed, the cargo would be transferred into carts drawn by horses and taken to the limekiln.

Unloading at Appledore
With kind permission of the artist Michael Lees

In his oil painting *Unloading at Appledore*, Michael Lees depicts the unloading of limestone from the vessel *Lucy* whilst she is grounded on the beach near the lifeboat slip at Appledore. Michael shows clearly the gaff being used, and the mawn baskets loaded with the stone being placed in the cart. Women from West Appledore were employed to load and unload the baskets and return them to the hold of the vessel. The *Lucy* was a small vessel of some 25 registered tons and was built at Bideford in 1871. There is also a picture of the *Lucy* on the beach at Bucks Mills by Michael Lees, but here, because conditions were particularly treacherous, a vessel would only stay for one tide. This would give just enough time for the limestone (or coal) cargo to be unloaded directly on to the beach. The carts would have to be loaded from the beach and, if the cargo was not fully moved by the time the tide came in and covered the load, the transfer of the cargo to dry land would continue after the tide had receded!

At Appledore, the soft shale rocks off the shore were worn away over the years due to wear from the wheels of the carts leaving the beach. These tracks are still visible today, and another set of tracks can be seen leading from the limekiln along the upper part of the beach to the slipway and along the road that passes the lifeboat house. Around the corner is the little bay known locally as 'Arry 'Inks (Harry Hinks was a well-known ship- and boat-builder in the area), which is part of the mud and sand foreshore known as Skern. Large wooden ships were brought to be broken up here and, if in good condition, much of the timber was reused. Children who are now of 'a certain age' used this area as a playground: the old limekiln was a 'fort' and the ships were the great pirate ships which scoured the Seven Seas for treasure and Dead Man's Chests – much more fun than watching a screen!

Slate from Port Madoc; coal from the Welsh ports in the Bristol Channel; bricks from the port of Bridgwater, all carried as bulk without the niceties of being stacked onto pallets. During unloading, bricks were tossed from the hold in blocks of six or nine to a crewman standing on the deck – with only momentum holding them together. The crewman in turn tossed them to a man on the quayside, who would place them in a cart. If there was a dolly winch available this made the work easier but even so, as the cargo was unloaded, the chap in the hold had to throw the bricks further and further up to the chap on the deck, and if the tide was ebbing the chap on the deck had to throw them further up to the man on the quay!

Some cargos, such as grain, flour or meal, were bagged in strong, closely woven hessian sacks, each sack weighing about a hundred-weight (around 51Kg) when full. Stone too was carried in the holds of some of the larger ships. Ships returning from foreign countries without a 'proper' cargo would be loaded with stone to give the ship ballast – a ship will sail and handle better if there is weight in the hold. If the owner was lucky, he might have been able to sell some suitable stones to a local builder.

The Breakwater at Appledore was the site in the estuary where these stones were discharged on to the beach, and over the years it built up such a high beach that today it is covered over and used as a car park. Before the Breakwater was tarmacked, university students came down to Appledore during the summer break to study and take samples of the stones which had been deposited there in the late 19th and early 20th centuries. Some of these stones originated from remote parts around the coasts of South America, and the students would have been very lucky to ever see them in their lifetimes.

Old photographs of Appledore quay show many of these vessels, either waiting for a cargo to be loaded, waiting to be discharged of cargo, or waiting for the tide so that they could sail. Others would be at anchor or on buoys in the area known as the Pool at the mouth of the two rivers just off the lifeboat slip.

The beach off Appledore quay was conducive to the maintenance of the bottoms of these vessels. From time to time hulls would need to be scraped free of marine growths – green weed and barnacles. It is surprising how much drag this growth can inflict and therefore slow the progress of the craft. Vessels that were moored alongside the quay were positioned on the ebbing tide so that one side of the hull would be tilted and exposed – a process called careening – allowing the crew and perhaps one or two other men to clean and tar the bottom. On the next tide the vessel would be canted the other way for the other side of the hull to be treated. This was a much cheaper way of getting the bottom cleaned than going into a dry dock for the work to be done.

Photographs with kind permission of the Appledore Historical Society Archives
In the foreground of the top photo is the clinker built boat Mona, which belonged to Bill Bailey, mentioned in the fishing chapter.

■ The Bessie Ellen: a West Country Schooner

Bessie Ellen is one of Britain's last wooden coasting ketches still under sail. Along with nearly 700 other West Country trading ketches she plied the waters around England and Ireland carrying a variety of cargoes. She was built in Plymouth in 1904 by W. S. Kelly specifically for the Newfoundland salt fish trade, but before she was launched the North Atlantic cod fishing bonanza had collapsed. She remained on the stocks until 1907, when she was purchased and launched by Captain John Chichester of Braunton, North Devon, who named her Bessie Ellen after his two daughters.

During the 1920s skippers from Appledore were in charge of her. One of these captains was my grandfather, Walter Henry Ford, who, along with his son (my father), also Walter Henry, sailed on her for several years. The photo below shows, from left to right: Walter Henry Ford Jnr., Mr Jack Chichester, the eldest son of the owner, and Captain Walter Henry Ford Snr. on the deck of the Bessie Ellen.

On the deck of the Bessie Ellen: mid 1920s

The Bessie Ellen discharge certificate of W. H. Ford (Junior)

During the war years, being too small to be used in service as a barrage balloon vessel (overall length 36.5 metres), she continued to carry cargo on the coastal trade until 1947, when she was sold to a coastal trader named Captain Moller, in Denmark. She continued trading in the Baltic until 1970 when she was laid up because she was too small to carry financially viable cargoes. From 1971 to 1983 she was owned by Ole Peitersen, whose intention it was to convert her as a charter vessel. He was able to complete all of the main structural work, but he retired from the project, covered her up with large tarpaulins, and put her on the market. In 2000 the Bessie Ellen was purchased by her present owner, Nikki Alford.

After three years of very hard work, Nikki brought the Bessie Ellen home to Plymouth after fifty-six years. Here the Bessie Ellen had new masts stepped, a bowsprit fitted and generally brought up to the required standard for sailing in British waters. Today she is used for a hands-on sailing experience for holidays or sail training. The former cargo hold has been transformed into a large saloon and dining area, with comfortable bunks.

The Bessie Ellen under sail after her refit
Photo by kind permission of Nikki Alford

In 2005 my husband and I were invited for a cruise on this old girl, and I was asked to cook the traditional meal of Schooner on the Rocks (*see Chapter 6*) for the crew and the other passengers. The meal was prepared in a very well equipped galley using belly pork, onions, sage and, of course, floury potatoes. It went in the huge oven and I was assigned a nice young man to lift the dish out of the oven when need be. On this particular day we were taking part in the Brixham trawler race so we were in the company of the sailing trawlers *Provident* and *Vigilance*. It was blowing force 6, gusting 7 to 8, and we were doing 7 knots: alas, the two sailing trawlers won the day, but I do not suppose that they had a plate of Schooner on the Rocks to enjoy at the end of a very arduous day! Everyone thoroughly enjoyed the meal and wanted the recipe and Bessie Ellen now uses this recipe as one of the meals provided for her guests to give them a flavour of life on a typical coasting vessel.

Life on board a West Country schooner, then, is still available to those who want to experience what life was like under the days of sail – but not under such arduous conditions as in the past! Bessie Ellen is equipped with a very modern Volvo Penta 6 cylinder, 265 Kw engine, but hauling the halliards and taking a turn on the wheel will require some muscle and stamina.

The author preparing Schooner on the Rocks in the galley of the Bessie Ellen

Chapter 4

Some Appledore sayings

■ *A language of their own*

Indigenous Appledorians have always had a language of their own – words and sayings that were part and parcel of village life – and it was best heard in the market. The market was the heart of Appledore. It was here that fresh supplies of meat, poultry, eggs, butter and, of course, 'a quaarter of craim' could be purchased on Wednesdays and Fridays. The market was the place where you heard the latest news, embellished and sometimes denied, but most of all it was a social gathering for the ladies of the town – from both west Appledore (originally the hamlet of Irsha), and Point. Sadly, in the 1960's the market was demolished and a restaurant, *The Port Quarter,* built in its place. Now that building has been turned into flats.

Plaque to mark the site of Appledore Market, on a fragment of the orginal wall in the garden of the Appledore Maritime Museum

The following are some of the stories that have been related to me over the years, as spoken in the Appledore dialect, and which would have been commonly 'exchanged' between the ladies in the market.

■ "Knawing looks"

If there had been visitors to the village market at that time listening to some of these conversations between the womenfolk they would have probably been at a loss to understand the gist of the subject. Not only would the intonation of the words have seemed strange but word usage and facial expressions also plays a large part in what is called a 'knawing look'.

No formal greeting was made if a family friend was seen: the conversation would start almost where it had been left off from when the pair had last met. A typical conversation would probably gone along the lines of:

'Yer, you knaw I said to 'ee last week that our maid won too wull [well]: wull I took her over to see Doctor Desmond.'
'What did he say about the maid?' the other would ask.
'Wull, he did'n think that there was too much to get bothered about as t'was probably to do with her age, but he did sound her all over.'
'What age is you maid then?'
'Wull, hers coming up to thirteen.'
'Yes,' said the other, 'it's all probably due to the same.'

The maid's mother might have told her friend that her maid had been 'blaking off' [fainting], but that 'Doctor Desmond had said that 'er would graw out of it'. The appellation 'maid' would be applied to a daughter or unmarried woman, and the expression 'all to do with the same' is one that fits any age group of the female gender. All through life, from being a child to post-menopause, it was always a case of 'it's all to do with the same', especially when a group of ladies were talking, and of course it would have been accompanied with a knawing nod and wink! And there were amongst the ladies of the town several who were great exponents of this 'art'! Comedians Les Dawson and Roy Barraclough with their Ada and Cissie sketches are always a reminder of the Appledore ladies doing their nodding and winking and knawing looks.

■ *Gowold [gold] and diamonds*

Nellie's man (husband) had been dead for several years. Someone saw her down on the Market hill one morning when Nellie was out getting her arrants (errands). She had not seen Nellie for a very long time and enquired how she was getting on.

> 'I'm getting on fine, me 'anse,' replied Nellie. 'I can have a bottle of beer and a fag whenever I like now without being chittered at, but there, it was always a waste of a good chitter an' when he did chitter, I wood'n take no notice ov'en.'

> 'You wood'n have another man then Nellie?' her friend inquired.

> Nellie looked her friend in the eye and replied 'I wood'n have another man even if his ass was gilded in gowold and studded in diamonds' and walked off! [The expression 'me 'anse' is a term of endearment and a corruption of 'me (or my) handsome'. And 'chitter' is chatter.]

■ *Not too wull [well]*

> ' 'em seed ee for a couple of weeks,' Maggie's friend said when she saw her on the quay.

> 'No,' replied Maggie, 'I've bin very ill. I felt proper bad with the diarrhoea and sickness. I felt as though I was dying from me middle both ways. Must have been they mussels 'e brought home t'other day. I must say it knocked the stroil [body strength] out of me for a day or two, but I've picked up again now. And I've told 'e not to bring 'ome any more ov they bleddy mussels.'

■ *Where be gwain [going]?*

Sarah was out for a walk delivering a piece of red hake [salmon], the result of last night's poaching excursion by her husband. The customer lived in the hamlet of Diddywell. She had gutted and washed the 'hake', dried it, and wrapped it in a clean white cloth before placing it in the bottom of her old wicker basket. Placed over this was some arrants [shopping] just to make it look as though she had been shopping in the grocery shop at the beginning of Irsha Street. Half way along the Lines she spotted Millie, the local gossip who had the reputation of even talking to a cat if she thought it had any gossip.

> 'Bugger,' Sarah thought, 'I'll have to cook 'er up an old yarn.' Millie called out, 'Where be gwain?' Quick as a flash Sarah said, 'Up round, down round and back round, Ansells and Ruckidown, where be you gwain?' and walked on.

Millie was known in the town as being a 'bitter weed' as she never had a good word to say about anyone. This expression is still used today by locals when describing someone unpleasant.

■ *Shivering and shaking...*

It was midwinter and bitterly cold, but Sid had laid some spillers (long fishing lines) on Sprat Ridge. There were some fine cod being caught and the bait he was using was sand eels, which he had caught back in the summer using his sprat net. He had then frozen them down in bags of twenty so that he would know how many he had in each pack when it came to baiting the lines in the dark. Before families had freezers, sand eels were dug out from the gravel/sand close to where the lines were being set, using either the hands or an old garden spade during the daylight hours. The coming of the freezers meant that the sand eels could be caught during the summer months using a sprat net. The net was a very much smaller version in both size and mesh size than that of the traditional salmon net, but it was deployed in the same way.

Twice a day Sid would have to go over to the ridge in his boat to tend the lines. This involved removing any fish that had been caught, clearing seaweed that had become entangled on the line and re-baiting the hooks. These lines were anchored to the ridge by long iron stakes driven into the sand that had been used by generations of fisherman. The lines would be stretched between these with perhaps twenty or so hooks attached to the main line by a length of line that is called locally, a zid.

At this time of the year there were cod to be caught and the occasional sea bass and thornback: thornback being the local general term for skate. Sid had had a good catch and had cleaned the line, re-baited the hooks, and the fish had been put into a hessian bag and carried to the boat. He rowed across the estuary to the beach on the Appledore side of the river on the flood tide and walked slowly up the gut to the moorings. Suddenly a swirl of tide caught him unawares and before he knew what was happening he was under the water. By the time he had got himself up on to his feet again the boat had drifted away. Rushing to try to grab the boat, he slipped again and received another soaking. Once he had got the boat on to the moorings he was beginning to feel the cold very badly. He picked up the bag of fish and walked up the beach to the slipway and walked along the street to his house where his wife was waiting up for him.

By then Sid was shivering and shaking with the cold [in Appledore language another common saying was 'bivvering with the cold']. When his wife saw him she exclaimed, 'Sid, you'm shivering and shaking like a dog shitting razor blades, I'll make ee a 'ot cup ov tay to waarm ee up!'

■ Ride to Barnstaple

Billy was down on the beach in his salmon fishing boat mending his net. He had got his net-mending needles loaded with twine and had pulled out the net to find the rips. He had just finished mending the first rip and put his hand in his pocket for 'his knive (knife), and 'twon there'. Just then his mate John came along the beach and Billy asked if he could borrow his knife. John took out his knife, opened it and handed it handle first to Billy. Billy tried to cut the twine which he was using to mend the net with but the blade was too blunt. 'You could ride to Barnstaple on that one,' said Billy, 'and it wood'n scratch your ass.', and handed back the knife, adding, 'I'll go 'ome and get me own.'

A well-known expression used by seamen about those who did not carry a knife, which to them is a most important piece of equipment, was 'a man without a knife is like taking a mermaid for a wife'. And to a seaman, that says it all.

■ Who do 'er think 'er is?

Often maidens from Appledore would go away into service: that is, they went into a large house as a maid. These jobs often came available because their elder sister or some other relative had recommended them to the lady of the house. Mary Ann had gone away to work in one of these posts. She had been away from home for at least a year before she came back to the village, and in that time she had, of course, learnt to 'spake proper'. This did not go down at all well with Mary Ann's friends, who were heard to say after they had met up with her down on the quay and had been speaking to her, 'Who do 'er think 'er is? Coming 'ome yer she-ing and we-ing. Anybody would think 'er was Lady Muck.'

■ All hot and hot

'I could smill (smell) they loaves of braid (bread) down on the Market heel (hill),' said Rosie as she entered the bakery shop in Bude Street. 'They'm smilling 'ansome.'

'Yes,' said the shop assistant, 'they'm just out of the awven (oven) and they'm all hot and hot, like the old man buried his wive (wife).' (Meaning that he was in that much of a hurry to 'get the rids of her' he buried her before she was cold!).

Rosie grinned and said, 'Wull then I'll have a round and a brown and a Nimble for our Kate. And while you'm at it I'll have a couple of they there fairy knubbies for our tay, them looking 'ansome. Aw, and I nearly forgot I'll have an ounce of 'east (yeast). I shall rub up a couple of 'east cakes at the weekend.'.

'Knubbies' are a type of fairy cake with currants or sultanas: the 'k' is sometimes pronounced and sometimes silent. Knub is a 16th-century precursor for the modern day 'knob' which has been retained in the Appledore dialect: so in today's lingo they might be 'knobby cakes'!

■ That's an 'ansome cheel you've got there...

Old Sarah was often seen pushing a pram around the streets of the village and, at times, on the road to Northam and Bideford. Everyone knew that, in Appledorian parlance, that she had neither 'chick nor cheel', which meant she had no children or grandchildren. The old-style prams had a false bottom in which mothers could carry clean terry towelling nappies and other baby requirements: needless to say, Old Sarah carried her stock of red hake around in this compartment, and the cheel was a very realistic doll bundled up so that it could not be recognised as such by anyone looking into the pram!

Very often old Sarah would be stopped by people who did not know what was the true content of the pram and say, 'there's a 'ansome cheel you've got there – niver makes a sound'. To which Sarah would reply, 'Aye, he's an ansome cheel zackly like ees father, but I've got to dap on now afore he wakes up.' And would hurry off to deliver a bit of red hake to her customers.

■ Which way is the wind blowing?

In the days of sailing vessels the most important factor to the mariner was the speed and direction of the wind. On occasion, vessels would be confined to port for days or even weeks on end because of adverse weather conditions. This meant that if the vessel was not trading there was no income for both the vessel's owners and the crew. It was at these times that the expressions 'If I haven't got hake I'll have herring', or 'tis low water' were used rather than saying I have no money.

When the wind was being particularly variable in direction which required the sails to be constantly trimmed and reset, the seamen often said ''tis up and down the mast like Paddy's hurricane'.

Mary Duck was a unmarried lady of very short stature and slight build but the life she followed had made her tough and resourceful as a great many ladies of the village were. As an unmarried lady she had to make a living along with the widows who had lost their husbands early in their lives and had not remarried.

She lived in one of the cobbled courts in Irsha Street consisting of one room up, one room down and one out the back. She made a living by scraping the beach, digging cockles in the summer and in the depths of winter she and three or four other ladies would pick laver (a type of edible seaweed – there is more on this subject in chapter 5) from the pebble beds at the back of Northam Burrows. They would walk out across the Burrows and down across the beach in all 'wets and weathers', carrying the large maun baskets which they would fill with laver. On one particular day the wind was blowing very strong and it got up under her long skirts and lifted poor Mary – who was only built like a rish light – up into the air and then deposited her on the pebbles several yards away. From then on if there was a gale of wind blowing and it was carrying away any articles that were not fixed or lashed down firmly it was said to go up in a 'Mary Duck's whirlwind'.

[A 'rish light' is either a bunch of marram grass or rush which may have been gathered from the Burrows, coated a few times with tallow and used as a light instead of a candle. And a maun or maund basket was a wide-mouthed willow basket (see the photograph on page 42). A row of old pollard willows in the fields bordering Northam Burrows are said locally to have been used for making such baskets.]

Mary lived in a very small cottage, which she would paint and decorate herself. But in her old age she had to rely on friends and neighbours to help her out ,which they did gladly. A young lady who lived along from Mary in Irsha Street was asked to paper her front room. Mary told the young lady 'to stick that there paper as close to the wall as you ken as me room is small enough'.

■ Lily White

As was the custom in many other parts of the country, washing day was on a Monday. The fire would have been lit under the copper, which had been filled with water and brought up to temperature, and then the clothes put in and boiled up. Into this water would have been put either washing soda crystals or soap flakes. Very often the soap flakes would have been made by shaving blocks of soap with a sharp knife. Alternatively, hot water was dipped out of the copper into an oval-shaped galvanised tin bath and the clothes hand-washed with the aid of a scrubbing board and a whole block of hard soap.

A 'dipper' was a small galvanised bowl with a wooden handle used for many tasks around the home and at the workplace: it was used as a bailer to dip out water that had accumulated in fishing boats; and farmers and seafaring families who kept poultry used a dipper to measure out corn or meal (the coarse ground edible part of grain) which was often mixed with the vegetable waste which had been boiled up to be fed to the fowls. Appledore men often scavenged corn or meal from the holds of the sailing vessels. Corn was transported in large hessian sacks and often a sack or two would have been torn or chaffed, leading to spillage. A friend of the captain of the vessel would be asked to sweep out the hold, and although a very dusty job it was well worth the effort and discomfort as it would produce enough feed for perhaps several months.

The rinsing of clothes was carried out in another galvanised bath filled with cold water. If sheets were being washed then a Reckitts Blue Bag (a patent chemical formula containing ultramarine and baking soda) was put into the rinse water so that the sheets would be made whiter.

Wringing out the washing was most often done by hand, but sometimes by mangles with great wooden rollers and ironwork, although these were few and far between. The clothes were put on clothes lines made with tall posts (often old ships' spars) and a wire line. The whole lot of the washing was pulled to the top of the post with a rope and pulley and the rope made fast around a wood or metal cleat attached to the post. Because the large families of the time resulted in great heaps of washing, these clothes lines were rigged in such a way that two lines of washing could be hung out at once. These very substantial clothes lines were made by seamen to withstand heavy duty work and strong winds. Appledore womenfolk would often refer to the washing as 'giving it a watter'. If for some reason the washing had become smeeched (smudged) with soots or blacks from the chimneys it did not seem to bother them, because the saying then was 'Wull if tid'n lily white, tis honey sweet', meaning that even if it is not too clean at least it smells better.

On days when the clothes did not dry quickly and the air was damp, the ladies would say that there was 'not much dry'th up', and days when there was mist or drizzle on the wind, the conditions were said to 'be giving or 'tis giving'. And the same expression was also used when the ice began to melt after a prolonged cold spell.

Appledore laver pickers: left, Mary 'Duck' Jewell; centre, either Bella Down or Mammy Trick; right, Sarah Ann Pile (*Seaweed gatherers at work*, Beaford Old Archive Images©, Beaford Arts)

Making cawch with orts

Nothing was ever thrown away in Appledore. If there were any scraps of food which had been around for that long that they had become inedible to the family, they were boiled up and given to the fowls or the pig. I can still recall the smell of cod's heads and guts which were being boiled up on the Bodley stawve (stove) which, not having been watched 'in a proper manner' had boiled out over the edge of the saucepan and on to the stawve: we called it essence of cod!

On the right-hand side going up Bude Street there is a covered alleyway, at the end of which there are a couple of cottages and a small courtyard. These days the door to this entrance is closed and the frontage gives the impression that it is a dwelling, but it is an entrance to what was known to the locals who lived around this area as 'pegs (pigs) bucket alley'. The reason being that the lady and her husband who lived there kept pegs in their walled garden at the top of One End Street, and the buckets were there for the neighbours to 'empt (empty) any orts (leftovers) or teddy skins (potato peelings) into. This mixture was boiled up and fed to the pegs. When the pegs were killed, the neighbours were offered some of the meat at a very reasonable price.

At least one day a week there was a meal known as a cawch. This was a feed made out of the remains or 'orts' of a very large joint of meat or a fowl that had stopped laying and was not viable to keep and had been killed and made into a meal. Left over vegetables grown in the garden or allotment were added together with stock, and sometimes suet dumplings, boiled and then simmered on the Bodley stawve until it was time for the meal. Alternatively, there would have been cottage pie, the meat having been minced in a machine clamped to the table. Potatoes, also from the garden, were used as the topping. Seasonal vegetables such as spring cabbage, sprouts, carrots, runner, kidney or broad beans, also from the garden, were usually served with the pie.

Then there was 'cawch surprise'. This dish would contain all the savoury orts from the safe (outside larder) with potatoes, carrots, swede and onions – Appledore people always loved their onions! Over the top of this was placed a tarpaulin of pastry, either suet or short crust. As our mothers' used to say: 'tis all filling, if tid'n fattening'. This meal was referred to as orts pie.

■ When 'tis brown 'tis cooked

Bena always made 'ansome knubbies. So when her newly married young neighbour came in and asked her about a cake made from a packet mixture she didn't quite understand. Cakes and knubbies was always made using flour, margarine, eggs (from the 'vowls' up the garden) sugar and a very secret ingredient. Bena's neighbour understood what had to be done to make up the mixture, but the instructions had omitted the length of time the mixture had to be in the awven (oven) plus the temperature the awven had to be set at. Bena being a practical sort of woman told her neighbour to: 'put en in a medium awven, and when 'tis brown 'tis cooked but, when 'tis black 'tis buggered'!

■ Me ass was making buttons

John and his brother Henry had been out poaching for salmon. John had driven around to the spot where Henry had moored the boat, on the other side of the River Torridge at Instow. The car was driven down onto a small slipway alongside the main road so that it was out of sight of any patrolling police or water bailies (bailiffs).

Having made their way down across the beach to the little 14-foot boat constructed by a well known Appledorian family of boat builders specifically for poaching, the two men set off into the darkness. When they got to the main gut the last of the ebb was coming down and they deployed the net. John held on to the head rope whilst Henry guided the boat along at right angles to the tide with a pair of paddles. The boat and net stopped drifting and for several minutes everything was still. Then as the flood tide took a hold the boat and net started on the upstream flow. After a few moments the net came alive. The water was not very deep so the fish migrating upstream were in shallow water. Suddenly the net was almost pulled from John's hand and the splashing of water almost the length of the net could be heard. 'Hit the jackpot yer,' growled Henry. His brother agreed adding that he could hardly hold the net. By this time it was making a good flood tide and they had to haul the net into the boat. There appeared to be red hake (a poachers' name for salmon: see page 35) everywhere, splashing and tugging in the net. As John ailed (hauled) the net containing the hake in over the gunnel of the boat, Henry deftly removed them from the net and dispatched them with the priest. They had caught twelve red hake ranging from 8 to 15 pounds (4 to 7kg) in weight.

Tucked up under the stern sheets Henry always kept a couple of large hessian sacks; he kept them there just in case of such a night as tonight. The net was put back into its hessian sack and stowed away up under the stern sheets where Henry kept his spare bags. The two men washed the scales from the bottom boards of the boat with a piece of rag and lifted the bottom board in the stern and dipped out the water that had collected there. Returning to the beach the two men quickly moored the boat, grabbed a bag each and went up the beach to where the car was parked. John opened the boot and Henry placed the bags inside, covering them with a tarpaulin.

The car was driven up onto the road and was going along the straight when lights came up from behind. Henry had just put a roll-up in his mouth and was about to light it when John said, ' 'tis the police and they want us to stop.' John pulled into the lay-by and stopped. The policeman pulled up behind, got out of the car and walked over to them. John wound down his window to speak to the policeman.

As it was late November and there was a chilly dampness in the air, the brothers still had their oilskins on with the collars turned up and the policeman mistook the two men for the pilots who brought ships in over the notorious Bideford bar,

'You two pilots going around to Appledore?' he said. 'Yes,' they said. 'I think the wind is going to get up later on,', said the policeman, 'I hope it isn't going to be rough out over the bar for you tonight', and went back to his vehicle.

The pair let the policeman drive on and waved as he went by. Henry remarked to his brother that was a close one. 'Yes', said John, 'me ass was making buttons.' Henry lit his roll-up took a deep drag and let his mind drift to all those red hake in the boot of the car: they would bring in a fair few shilling, he thought.

■ 'Er was evil

'I don't knaw what the metter was with our Annie, somebody must ov upset 'er, 'er was evil, and when I asked 'er what the metter was 'er just took 'er ass in 'er hand and went off 'ome. I shall 'ave to spake to 'er in a day or dree (three) to find out what was the metter – after 'ers had time to cool down a bit.'

■ Will 'ee ave a cup ov stuff

When visiting a friend or a relative the first thing that always used to happen was that the black iron kettle would be pulled over to the hot part of the Bodley stawve so that it would come quickly to the boil. Whilst this was being done the person would be asked, or told, depending on the tone of voice 'would ee like a cup ov stuff?' Now, a cup of stuff could mean anything, a cup of tay, or cawffee and sometimes it would mean a cup of hot medicinal drink which contained a goodly number of fingers of alcohol! The alcoholic version was a drink which was often produced during wild cold weather. When inclement weather was lasting for several days the ladies would say 'yers a night ov weather this morning'.

Aunt Edie was a lady in the village who was always making 'a cup ov stuff' – the 'medicinal kind'! Often three or four times a day she would be seen nipping down around the corner of One End Street with her brown jug to the Coach and Horses pub in Market Street. Anyone calling in to see Aunt Edie would very often come out a bit wobbly on their legs after having a cup ov her stuff!

■ What did the salmon say to the sole?

Today the children of Appledore speak without much of the unique village dialect. But those who were children in the 1950's and still had relatives who spoke the dialect had the advantage of mixing with those old men and ladies from whom they were able to learn the village dialect words. Some boys would want to spend their time down on the beach with the menfolk, tending the boats and nets, and whilst learning how to mend a net or set a long line, or spiller as it was called, would also pick up the Appledore language. Other boys who were perhaps interested in learning the skills of the boat builder, would get an after-school and Saturday job in one of the many boatyards which were in back yards or at the bottom of the Courts in Irsha Street. Here they would learn the language and the skills of the boat builder and, if showing any promise, would be offered an apprenticeship on leaving school.

The maidens, on the other hand, would be expected to be learn from their mothers and grandmothers the business of home-keeping, cooking, sewing, knitting: socks knitted with Worsted wool which were used by the men to keep the feet warm inside the sea boots, and the famous Appledore frocks, which were knitted using five long steel needles and a leather tack, were mandatory skills to be learnt. Some maidens who did not have any brothers were sometimes both a son and daughter and learnt an assortment of skills such as growing vegetables, looking after chickens, painting a boat and roping a net. And it is mostly these children, now elderly adults, who are still carrying on the Appledore lingo as it as known.

Traditional Appledore frocks (sweaters) with steel needles, tack and notebook with wearer's measurements

So, it is of little surprise that the children of Appledore learnt swear words at a very early age. The words 'bleddy' and 'bugger' being the most used, although stronger words were often used by the menfolk but not in front of a young 'cheel'. By the intonation of the voice from an adult, the cheel would know whether or not he was being chided or it was being used as a term of endearment. 'You bleddy little heller' was a favourite used when a child had misbehaved.

Children learnt at a young age to recognise and name the different species of fish, to know a male crab from a female crab and at what time of the year to use these as bait for fishing. Even the peeling of the crab had to be done in a proper manner so that it was presented to the fish on the hook as naturally as possible. Grandfathers who were retired seamen but now spent their time fishing would teach the boys the skills they had picked up over their lifetimes. These old men had sayings they would often come out with to have a bit of fun with the cheel – the cheel being unaware of the joke that was being played. The grandpa would ask the cheel 'What did the sole say to the salmon?' And the cheel would answer 'Ah, salmon.' Then the grandpa would ask 'What did the salmon say to the sole?' And the cheel would answer innocently 'Ah sole'! Thus the cheel would be introduced to the subtle art of swearing!

■ A sample

A sample in Appledorian speech is a word that is often used to express dismay about a happening or about something someone has done that is not considered the correct thing to do. It is a corruption of the word 'example' and was used to describe the person who had misbehaved as being 'a sample of all that is wrong', or if the misdemeanour was really bad the expression would be 'what a bleddy sample' – and it is still used quite frequently today.

■ Widdy Waddy

This expression was often used to describe someone who was being indecisive or, having made up their mind to do a thing, would then persist in keep on changing it by putting excuses in the way so that a decision would not to be made by them.

Chapter 5

Fishing the Taw and Torridge estuary

■ *Looking to the sea: time, tide and sustenance*

The residents of Appledore have always looked to the sea for food, and fishing with hook and line or a net was a means of obtaining food for the family, or indeed of bringing in a few shilling. But the rhythms of the sea also told them the time. Many households in the village in the early twentieth century did not have a clock. We were fortunate in having an old kitchen clock which my granny had paid thirty shillings for. It should have cost two pounds but it did not chime! She had bartered with the clock maker and had the price reduced by ten shilling!

Very few men in the village had a pocket watch and wrist watches were not even contemplated by men who had their hands in and out of the water as they went about their business of making a living. The men would often congregate on the sea side of the road outside the Seagate Hotel from where they could observe both the church clock which struck the hour and the ebb and flow of the tide at the confluence of the Taw and Torridge rivers: from these observations they would calculate the time of the next high or low water.

Often as a cheel I would be sent down to the quay to see where the tide was. I would run home and tell father that Mr Cox's boat was 'just taking the ground' if the tide was ebbing, but if it was flood tide I would report that the tide was 'just around the toe of the rock', or Mr Cox's boat was 'just fleeting'. With this information he would look at our kitchen clock and calculate the time of the next high or low water,

Top: off Appledore Quay at low water
Bottom: high water 6 hours later

adding in the day-to-day variants and weather conditions. So, in the same way that the old residents of the village would know the time by the daily ebb and flow of the tide, it was known as Appledore time or tide 'ee time (the right tide for you (you = 'ee' in dialect)): both these 'times' referred to the time when the tide was right to go fishing. The time of day at which the high water occurred also told them whether they were neap or spring tides.

'Shipyard time' at Richmond Dock...

Appledore time was also kept by the working hours of the busy Richmond Dock. The day started with the 7.30 a.m. hooter; it would be sounded again at 10 a.m. for the 15-minute mid-morning break, and then again for the return to work. At 12.30 p.m. the hooter sounded for the hour-long lunch break, and again promptly at 1.30 p.m. At the sound of the lunchtime hooter there would be a rush of men from the dock to their homes in Appledore where, on arrival at home, a cooked lunch would be waiting on the table. The afternoon tea break was unofficial and was taken surreptitiously out of the sight of the foremen behind a bulkhead or in any other cubby hole! Then at 5.30 p.m. the hooter would be sounded again for the home run. When the mass exodus of 80–100 men came out of the gates, either on foot or on bicycles, or iron horses as they were known, no one stood in the way. If the dock had a rush job on then the men whose skills were needed to complete the work within the contract time would work overtime until 6.30 p.m.

Most fishermen in the village would fish for about six hours – three hours on the ebb and three on the flood tide. If they did not catch anything in those six hours there was 'nort about', and if they'd been caught out in a sudden bout of bad weather and could not get back in to the harbour because there was insufficient water in the river to get to the moorings, and they had not caught any fish, then the expression was 'all I got was a wet ass and 'ungry guts'.

The nature of the Taw and Torridge estuary dictates that the tide times between half ebb and half flood are the best for fishing. But if there were excursions out over the bar to catch skate or turbot with long lines then the crossing of the shallow bar had to be added to the equation: if the wind was blowing against the tide this would make crossing hazardous, both for going out over the bar or coming back in, especially at low water, when perhaps there would only be a few inches of water under the keel of the boat.

■ Seasonal fishing

The seasons also played an important role in the activities of fishermen. The summer months were the time for bass fishing and going across the bar. Long lines were laid in the sandy areas to the south of the bar to catch skate and turbot. Bass and mackerel were usually caught by towing a lure or baited hook behind the boat: when these fish feed they are very close to the surface as they force the whitebait (brit) to the surface. The line therefore did not require any, or very little, weight on it. There are marks (favoured fishing spots) where bass could be caught while at anchor, but after that particular mark had been fished a few times it had to be left alone for a while so that more fish would move back in: nature abhors a vacuum.

Before the advent of rubber eels, fishermen would make their own lures which would be towed behind the boat on a long length of line, sometimes with spiral weights attached to take the bait down to the fish. Before inboard and outboard engines the fishermen used a lug sail or paddles to propel the boat. If the bass were in an area which was too shallow, and therefore dangerous, the boat would be anchored in a safe spot off this area, and using a method known locally as 'whiffing', the fisherman would cast into the surf or shallow rocky area where the fish were feeding. These lures were hand-crafted out of the white underside skin of a sole (*Solea solea*). The skin was peeled from the fish and hung

Left: sole skins cut and left out to dry
Right: the finished lure with hook and skin

up to dry in a shed or outhouse until it was crisp. The fisherman would then select the hooks he wanted to use and with a pair of sharp scissors would cut from the sheet of sole skin a mirror image shape of a brit. This would then be folded in half, with the scales on the outside, and sewn with thread on to the hook, ensuring that the scales would appear as they would on a fish – smooth from the head towards the tail. After a short time of being in the water the skin would become pliant again and shine as brightly as it did on the living fish. If a silver-coloured hook was used this would also help to enhance the attraction to the fish, usually a hungry sea bass, and was a most successful lure.

■ Whiffing

The art of whiffing is very similar to that of fly fishing. A fly rod and reel was used but the lure was sole skin, and often two hooks were used with a double swivel. The two leaders were of different lengths and were cast into the sea in the same manner as in the fly fishing technique, then slowly reeled back towards the boat, which was either at anchor or drifting with the tide. Fishing this way was only used when the bass were on the surface feeding on the brit. For me, the adrenaline rush when there were two bass on the line was incredible: having two fish, with perhaps a combined weight of 5 or 6 pounds (around 3 kilos), swimming in different directions on a light rod needed all the skills that the fisherman/woman possessed to bring them to the dip net.

There was an old Appledorian fisherman named Bill Bailey who was most proficient at the technique of whiffing. He would often be seen out in the estuary fishing for bass in his clinker-built boat, Mona, at the confluence of the Taw and Torridge rivers known as the String, usually on the flood tide. Bill would use a lug sail or paddles for propulsion; it was not until his latter years that he employed the use of a Seagull outboard engine.

Today, a similar technique is used, but it is called bubbling. A small plastic bubble is filled with water to give it weight, and a rubber eel, which looks similar to a sand eel, is used as a lure. The tackle used is an 8 or 9 foot long fibreglass rod with either a multiplier or a spinning reel. The lure is cast out into the tide and then drawn slowly back to the boat. Fishing this way can be performed from either a boat or the shore. If the angler is on the shore, a long beach-caster rod is used and a spinning or multiplier reel.

■ *Sieving watter*

During the summer months the licensed salmon fishermen would be in favoured and historic berths, or draughts, along the shore line of the estuary. These men often worked the mid-tide system (fishing 2–3 hours before low water and returning 2–3 hours before high water). Originally, the ropes and salmon nets would have been made of cotton, and to preserve this natural fibre before being made up into a complete

Bill Bailey in his boat, Mona (c.1960s)
Photo with permission of Ronald Slade, Appledore Historical Society Archivist

net it would have been put through the process of barking, a very similar process to the tanning of hides. These cotton nets and ropes were very heavy when wet.

The fishing boats themselves were 18 feet long, clinker built with larch and oak, and some of the local fishermen would sometimes request elm for the gunnels. There would be four men to a boat: three in and one ashore. They would row out, two men pulling with paddles or oars and one man or boy heaving the net out over the stern: the fourth man standing ashore would be holding on to the shore rope. The net would be let out to form a semi-circle in the water and the three men in the boat would come ashore some distance from the man with the shore rope. One would walk to him and grab either the head or foot rope: the head rope is at the top of the net and floats on the surface of the water, held up by cork floats spaced at equal distances along it. The foot rope is at the bottom of the net and has lead weights similarly spaced. Then the four men would gradually walk towards each other, pulling in the net, and tightening the circle. Any fish caught in the net would be in the 'bunt' or bag. This activity was often known as 'sieving watter'!

With the advent of lighter nylon material for ropes and netting the boats became smaller and were made of fibre glass: 'plastic boats' father called them! This change from natural materials to synthetic meant the loss of a number of jobs in boat building and repairing in the village – there were a number of small family boat yards at the backs of the houses along the sea side of Irsha Street which made the wooden boats.

Also scattered around the village in the back yards of some fishermen's cottages and pubs – the one situated behind the Beaver Inn in Irsha Street springs to mind – were the great cauldrons under which a fire was lit and in which the cotton netting and ropes were barked. Great lumps of powdered bark were added to the water, stirred with an old paddle and then the items to be barked would be placed into the steaming cauldron and boiled. The ropes and bundles of netting would then be lifted out and hung up on lengths of old rope or pieces of timber to dry.

Winter was the time for fishing for cod and at some marks, dab, locally known as 'flooks' (flukes) – in local dialect the name rhymes with 'looks' not 'flu'. October, November and December are the favoured months for catching cod. Flooks enter the rivers at this time too, so that by the end of December or early January they can move up the rivers to the areas where they will spawn.

In late autumn – usually during November – the winter run of salmon begins and it was at this time that these fish were regularly poached by the Appledore fisher folk. Combining a bit of poaching with cod fishing was the norm. As cod are a bottom-feeding and deep-water-living species they were fished for with the boat at anchor, skilfully placed over the 'cod pits' as they were called, using known 'marks' on the land

Salmon fishers ready to shoot the 'Sunset' draught on Sprat ridge

which would give the angler a triangulation. Once anchored on the correct mark the line would be baited with crab (cod are not a fish that can be caught with lures in the Taw/Torridge estuary) which had been peeled and placed on the hook. To hold the line on the bottom a large lead weight was attached to the end of the line, and about 6 feet up from this there was a three-way swivel which joined the lead to the main line and the long (almost 20 feet) branch line known as a zid: at the end of which was the baited hook.

While holding the line or lines – because often two lines were used, one on the port side and one on the starboard side of the boat – patiently waiting for a bite, the fisherman would be watching all around him to see if there were any 'red hake' (salmon) jumping out of the water. If he did see any movement by these fish this would encourage him to pull in the lines and anchor and start the process of setting or shooting the net just before low water: drift nets were used, so named because they hang from the surface of the water to nearly the bottom like a curtain and drift with the tide. The fisherman used a pair of paddles to keep the boat in position at right angles to the net, with both the head and foot rope held in the hand, and if a fish hit the net it would be felt through these ropes. On the flood tide there was a better chance of catching a red hake because the fish would have the urge to move further up the estuary towards the source of fresh water and their spawning grounds.

Come Christmas when the really wild weather began, most fishermen would take their boats from the water to the safety of places set aside for them on the quay. At the beginning of March, and before Easter, the rule was that they had to be off the quay, but today boats seem to be on the quay year-round and are never put into the water. So the months of January, February and March were the 'lean' months and very often the crab bait would be scarce, though there would be an occasional year when there would be plenty of crabs about but no fish to catch, and then there would be years when there would be lots of fish but no crabs!

Early March, when perhaps a few crabs had been caught in the crab traps or when there were a few sand eels available which had been dug from the wet sand during daylight hours, a long line would be baited on Sprat Ridge to catch some late cod, known in the village as 'Marchies'. This exercise involved crossing the estuary twice a day to tend the lines and if conditions were favourable the drift net would be deployed in the hope of catching a red hake, which, of course, would be a bonus. If a salmon was caught and there were a few 'Marchies' about then the salmon would be put in the bottom of the hessian sack and the Marchies put on the top of it, so if the fisherman was stopped by the water bailie (bailiff) and he looked into the sack all he would see were the cod!

■ Fishing bait

Hook and line fishing requires bait, and for centuries the estuary of the Taw and Torridge rivers has provided the bait for fishermen. Sand eels (*Ammodytidae* and *Hypotychidae* families) are used as bait outside the bar in the areas where the seabed is sandy. The hooks of the long lines are baited with these creatures to catch skate and turbot.

A sand eel, known locally as a sprat

Lugworms (*Arenicola marina*) and ragworms (*Nereis diveriscolor*) are soft-bodied creatures best used for catching flooks. During the late autumn and early winter months when the flooks come into the river to spawn, anglers successfully use lugworms and ragworms as bait. Some fine flooks can be caught upstream in both the Taw and Torridge rivers at this time where the tidal currents are not as strong as those out in the estuary. But the most popular bait of all that is used in the estuary is the common shore crab (*Carcinus maenas*).

As its name suggests, the common shore crab can be found on the seashore all around the British Isles. It is found in a diversity of habitats: rocky shores; sheltered mud flats; and sandy beaches which have stones or rocky outcrops with a covering of brown seaweed. It is into the seaweed-covered cracks and crevices of the rocks and stones that the crab crawls to conceal itself until the tide returns, or night falls. Then the crab will emerge to prey on small invertebrates or scavenge for food. Shore crabs are very adaptable creatures, often found in estuarine salt marsh pools which contain water diluted by rain or land run-off, but also able to tolerate water with a higher saline level than 'normal' seawater.

Crabs are heavily predated, whether fully grown and being taken by humans, fish and birds, or in the planktonic larval stage when they are taken as food by plankton feeders such as fish and jellyfish. It is no wonder therefore, that at times there is a dearth of crabs, and this very often occurs when the fish are plentiful, which reminds me of the Fisherman's Prayer:

> *Sitting still and wishing,*
> *Makes no country great,*
> *The Good Lord sends the fishes,*
> *But you must catch the bait.*

An 'owler in aggressive posture showing its claws

An 'owler with an underlain in mating position

'owlers and pullers...

During the summer months the male or cock crabs are known as 'owlers and are often found with a female, or hen crab, clutched to their underside. Needless to say, they are very aggressive at this time as they are protecting their mates. The 'owler is much bigger than the female, his claws are very strong and can deliver a nasty nip – hence the name of 'owler! For the few weeks that she is being protected and carried around under him the female is known as an 'underlain'. After moulting her hard shell she is known as a 'puffy', and while she is in this state the pair will mate. But it is when she is in this soft state that she is also considered to be a 'deadly' bait for catching sea bass.

The female crab moults during the summer months, and the male crab in the autumn. The difference between the moulting seasons is related to mating. A male's underbelly, with the sperm-producing organs, is narrower than that of the female's, which has to expand to enable the growth of her eggs. As the eggs develop, they swell and push this part of the shell away from the body. In this state she is said to be 'in berry'. The eggs are carried around attached to the female's abdomen until they hatch and the larvae are released into the sea to become part of the planktonic life in the ocean. After several moults the larvae become recognisable as crabs.

In late autumn or early winter 'owlers become less aggressive and dig themselves into the sand or mud and prepare to moult. It is during this process that they are used for bait. The fisher folk of Appledore have known about this seasonal change for hundreds of years, and have used the crab's instinct to bury itself by providing a ready made home for it to crawl into. These are known as crab-traps and are nothing more than pieces of iron guttering or ridge tiles laid on sandy or slightly muddy beaches. The traps are set across the flow of the tide to prevent water rushing into the trap and disturbing the crab. During this period, just before the moult, the 'owlers are known as 'pullers'.

■ Winter fishing and the 'fresh'

Winter fishing for cod is always the time for the fishermen to set the crab traps for the pullers. Cod congregate in the deep water pits in the estuary and crab is always the favourite bait because, unlike lugworm or ragworm, it stays on the hook in fast-flowing currents. Fishing for cod is always more successful on the ebb tide; but after heavy rain in the Exmoor and Dartmoor catchment areas of the Taw and Torridge rivers, fishing can be successful on the flood tide at one or two favourable marks. At these marks some very large cod used to be caught. Locally, this flood water coming down from the moors is known as a 'fresh'.

Crab traps set on a beach of mixed sand and mud

The fresh would also bring downstream anything that had been lying on the bankside or in the water meadows alongside the river. Large pieces of trees, and branches that had fallen or been lopped would all be carried down the rivers to the estuary and deposited at the high water mark. We would gather this flotsam and take it home for fuel. Using the anchor, the boat would be secured at the tide line, which would usually be very close to the low water mark, and the lengths of wood were then carried to the boat; not an easy task, especially in the places where the sand was wet and 'sinky'. After gathering the driftwood, father and I would cut the longer pieces into lengths of about 3 foot using a large bow saw. The diameter of the wood varied from 6 to 10 inches. After enough had been cut I would go up and down the beach with armfuls of wood, warming up in the process! Father would carry on sawing. The wood we found was mainly oak, elm and perhaps some ash.

It was also in winter that the drift net would be set, or shot, across the tide, usually about half an hour before low water. The boat and net would then slowly drift along with the ebbing tide; a pair of paddles were used to keep the boat and net across the tide. At low water both the boat and the net would come to a halt for quite some minutes before the flood tide would start to flow, bringing both the boat and the net gently back the way it came. Fishing this way is called drifting, and it was the method used to catch salmon and sea trout out of season. We always knew if there were any of these about, and therefore worthwhile to deploy the net, because we would watch for them leaping from the water while we were line fishing for cod.

■ Do 'ee want a bit ov red hake me 'ansome?

After there had been a successful night of sieving the watter, the fish were brought home and laid on a stone floor and covered with a wet hessian sack. Most of the cottages had either stone or wooden floors. Wooden floors were very often fashioned out of reclaimed ships' planking, supported on great bulks of timber that had also at one time been the timbers of a vessel. Stone floors were usually made with slate flags, or flaggings, brought across the Bristol Channel from Wales as cargo in the sailing vessels: sand was laid down to make a level base for these. In the morning the lady of the house would turn to and gut and cut up the red hake (salmon) into large steaks, wash and dry them, and then wrap each one up in a clean white cloth. Most households had a large wicker basket which was used for shopping – no plastic bags in those days! The pieces of red hake were placed in the basket and covered with a cloth. Then putting on a clean pinny (pinafore/apron) she would do the rounds to her customers.

Appledore is full of drangs (alleys) and opes ('ope' is probably a corruption of 'opening' – a narrow passage between buildings) and they were used as 'rat runs' for both the ladies selling the red hake and the men who had caught it. If the water bailie (bailiff) was around at night the women-folk would have a light showing from a window, this light would pass along from house to house as the bailie moved along. The men on the beach would then go along the beach in the opposite direction and climb up a ladder to a back yard or a small quay, then disappear into the maze of and drangs and opes and go back to their homes. During the day, when the ladies were out delivering the red hake to their customers they were always on the lookout for a policeman or a water bailie. Should one of these be spotted, then a set of signals to one another was used to warn of the presence of the long arm of the law. Alternatively, they would enter a customer's front door, do their business, then go out by the back door into the many opes and drangs.

■ *Caught dree...*

Before the days of financial help from government, families had to fend for themselves. While city dwellers earned a few shilling to supplement family income through their own talents and contacts, country dwellers lived off the natural supplies of the land: rabbit, hare, rook (young rooks made a good pie), wood pigeon and the occasional poached pheasant from the estate. Some country folk were also adept at tickling the indigenous brown trout from the many streams around the area.

St. Andrew's fish

St. Rule or Regulus was a priest of Patrae in Achaia (Greece) said to have arrived in Scotland in the 4th century, bringing with him the relics of St. Andrew. St. Andrew is usually depicted in Christian art as an old man with long white hair and a beard, holding the Gospel in his right hand and leaning on a staff with the cross of St. Andrew carved at the top. He was martyred around 70 AD on a saltire cross and is the patron saint of Scotland.

The festival of St. Andrew is observed on 30 November, and it is about this time that there is a run of salmon (*Salmo salar*) and the occasional sea trout (*Salmo trutta*) into the Taw/Torridge estuary. Local fishermen call the sea trout 'pugs'. They are not as plentiful as salmon and are therefore more expensive: some believe that the sea trout has a more delicate flavour and prefer it to salmon. This run is known locally as the 'St. Andrew's fish', and these latecomers to the rivers are desperate to travel upstream to the redds (shallow depressions in the river gravel) where they will spawn; indeed, some of these fish are so ripe and so ready to spawn that if handled roughly the eggs or milt will come away from the fish. By this time the bodies of the fish have undergone physical changes. In the male the lower jaw has grown hook-shaped – known as a kype – and the skin has turned a rusty-red colour. Changes in the female are not so pronounced – her skin changes to a dark brown or purple and the usually white belly changes to grey.

After spawning, the fish are said to be 'spent' and many of them die. Those that do survive and drift downstream are nothing but skin and bone, which is hardly surprising as they have not eaten for many months. Both male and female fish at this time are known as 'kelts', but locally they are usually referred to as 'backward fish'. Should one of these fish be caught it was always released to continue the long journey back to the feeding grounds in the north Atlantic (it is now a statutory offence to take kelts), where they will feed and recover, then repeat the long journey back to the river of their birth the following year, ready to spawn a new generation.

In Appledore, poaching for salmon and sea trout to supplement the family diet and income was a way of life. Young boys and, in some cases young maids, were taught the art of setting a drift net across the estuary channels at almost low tide: it was when the tide turned and the red hake began to move into the confines of the river that they would be caught in the net. These fishermen were always pleased if they caught one. But there was a saying among them which was 'us caught dree – two to sill (sell) and one to ate'. Selling two salmon was the equivalent of a week's wage, and having food on the table with the third salmon, which hadn't had to be paid for was, for them, like winning the lottery. Children of these poaching household were often heard to cry 'Not salmon again!'

A brace of salmon

Chapter 6

Appledore cooking

■ *The Bodley*

The Bodley stawve (stove), the main source of heating and cooking in the homes of Appledorians, was patented by James Bodley in 1802. It was designed mainly for cooking, but was also adapted over the years for heating.

It was not until the late 1960s or early 1970s that the Bodley stawve began to become obsolete as a source of heating and cooking. These stawves, which were made locally, were made of iron and consisted of a grate with an awven (oven) at the side. The grate could also be used as an open fire by removing part of the top of the grate and deploying what was known as a bonnet, which more likely than not had been created by a family member or friend who worked in the blacksmith's shop at Richmond Dock.

A number of cottages in the village did not have electricity until the late 1950s. Until then it was gas lights with the fragile mantles that after a certain number of hours would pop and the light would go out, creating a scramble among the occupiers of the household to find a candle or a bicycle torch so that a new mantle could be fitted. Often, only one room in the house had a gas light. The remaining rooms, if need be, were lit by an oil lamp. An Appledorian saying is 'in the parlour there is three: he, the parlour lamp and she' – two is company without a doubt, so the parlour lamp went out!

The use of gas in those days was regulated by a meter. A shilling (five pence) piece would be fed into the meter and would buy a portion of gas.

But often neighbours would dash in and ask 'have 'ee got a shilling for the gas?' as their supply was running out. Ladies of the household had an ear for when the gas supply was diminishing as the sound, either from the stove or the light, would alter slightly. Thus, in the middle of a cooking session it was always a good idea to have a spare shilling to hand, because if the gas supply was allowed to run out then the whole batch of cooking would be spoilt. Twelve old pennies would be swapped for a shilling piece with which to feed the meter.

Basic cooking would be undertaken both in the awven and on the top of the stawve if boiling was required. A large iron saucepan was used if pea soup, suet puddings – both sweet and savoury – and, of course, Christmas puddings, were being cooked. Two iron kettles were always kept on the top of the stawve, one quite large – probably holding about two to three quarts of water – and the other smaller and holding about three pints or so. This little one would boil up quickly if anyone dropped in and was offered 'a cup ov tay'. If the household had a garden then very often they kept fowls, so the teddy (potato) skins and other peelings were boiled up on the stawve along with any fish heads, bones, fins and skin. This mixture was drained into a bucket, a few handfuls of meal were added, given a good stir, and then fed to the fowls.

■ *Schooner On The Rocks*

This traditional Appledore dish was originally a method of cooking a meal at sea and was usually prepared by the ship's boy on coastal sailing vessels. It is still a form of cooking used today by many Appledorians as it produces a good, solid meal without any of the modern day *haute cuisine* techniques, or as we Appledorians say *'haute de cawch'*!

Coastal sailing vessels had a small version of the Bodley with a brass rail or 'fiddle' to prevent utensils from sliding off. A deep ash pan was fitted and the whole thing stood on a plinth of fireproof material. But,

Schooner on the Rocks

as they were wooden vessels, during very rough weather the fire in the stawve would be doused to reduce the risk of fire; but in good sailing conditions it was usually kept going continuously to ensure a ready supply of hot water for a brew, a facility for cooking – either on the top with a saucepan or frying pan, and in the awven for the Schooner On The Rocks – or any other dish that required an awven for cooking. The stawve was also a source of heat for drying wet clothes and keeping conditions comfortable for the crew. The ship's boy was responsible for tending the stawve and making sure that the large iron kettle was always full and that the stawve was well-stoked, especially in winter.

The main ingredients for the Schooner On The Rocks meal consist of a cheap cut of meat such as a piece of belly pork, a waistcoat (breast) of lamb or a piece of brisket. More often than not belly pork was used because, with the addition of sage and onions, it made a very tasty dish of food, and it was probably the meat from the pig that had been kept by the captain in his garden and had been fed with the family scraps!

Potatoes, onions and sage were the other main ingredients, all put into a large enamel dish: sage and onion at the bottom, then the potatoes, which if large were quartered (these are the 'rocks'), and then over the top was placed the Schooner – the piece of meat. Salt and pepper was added and some boiling water poured over, the dish was then covered with another similar sized dish (these days foil is often used) and then brought back to the boil on the top of the stawve and boiled further for a good few minutes before being transferred to the very hot awven, keeping the lid on. Here it was kept at the high heat for half an hour or so before the awven heat was allowed to cool slightly. This juggling of awven temperatures was a skill a ship's boy quickly learnt or there would be cries of 'when 'tis brown 'tis cooked, when 'tis black 'tis buggered' from the hungry crew! From time to time the boy, in between his other duties of helping to sail the ship, would go below to check on the water level in the dish. Water would be replenished with simmering water from the kettle on the top of the stawve. This way the meal could be kept in the awven for several hours, just gently cooking away, so that when the captain gave the word the boy would go below to put a pan of coal into the fire to raise the heat and remove the top cover from the meal for a while so that the crackling would become crunchy. If the crackling remained soft it was used as something the crew could chew which would 'stay' their stomachs (stop hunger pangs) until the next meal. Floury potatoes were always preferred for this type of baked dinner rather than waxy or close ones as they would absorb the goodness from the meat, and the water which had cooked the meal would be slightly thickened by them – there never was any gravy browning used, it all came out of the dish in which the ingredients had been cooked. A meal cooked in this fashion could be kept in the awven for hours so long as the water level was checked from time to time. Cabbage, swede or other seasonal vegetables would be served with the meal.

Potatoes, cabbage or any other vegetables left over from the meal would be put together into a large dish and, as they used to say, 'squat up' into bubble and squeak which, when accompanied by the remaining cold meat and perhaps fried eggs and homemade pickle (probably made by the wife of the captain or one of the crew) would be the supper. It was always the habit to cook more than was needed for a meal so that there would always be some 'orts' to provide the next meal without too much time having to be taken up with preparation.

■ *Yeast or saffron cake*

This old Appledorian recipe has been used for generations by the ladies of Irsha Street, and indeed it is still being used today by Appledore maidens who live away from the village. These cakes were often made at Christmas instead of, or as well as, a Christmas cake. As in all yeast cooking, the general ambience of the room needed to be warm. The kitchen with a Bodley stawve or Rayburn was ideal because the dough was put to prove either in front of the stawve or in the bottom oven, which was cool. Again, the stawve had to be regulated to keep a constant temperature, Rayburn stawves had a temperature gauge situated on the outside of the oven door, but Bodley stawves had a brass knob on the oven door and the cook would grasp the knob to assess the temperature of the oven: this, surprisingly, was quite an accurate way of gauging the temperature. After cooking, the cakes were left to cool on cake racks until completely cold. They were then wrapped in a clean linen or cotton cloth and stored in a tin or on a cool shelf until required. Often these cakes were made by the wives of the crew or the captain of the sailing vessels and were taken to sea by the mariners, thus making a pleasant change to the diet. If the cake became a little stale then the boy would use a long handled toasting fork and toast slices in front of the open door of the stove and, if available, scrape some margarine or, if really lucky, butter on to the slices.

Recipe: Saffron cake and Knubbies

Ingredients
1 lb plain flour
¼ lb self-raising flour
4 oz sugar
½ lb sultanas
½ lb currants
2 oz mixed peel
½ lb margarine
¼ lb lard
¼ pint milk
½ teaspoon mixed spice
1 oz yeast
2 eggs
Pinch of salt
Pinch of saffron if saffron cake is being made

Method
Rub all the dry ingredients together in a large mixing bowl then add the sugar and fruit, keeping a teaspoonful of sugar back to cream the yeast. When the yeast has been creamed add the tepid milk and the beaten eggs to the mixing bowl. Using the hands, mix into a dough, adding the yeast liquid until it has all been absorbed. The dough at this stage should not be too stiff. If a saffron cake is being made, the saffron should be soaked overnight in a cup with a small amount of hot water; this flavoured water can then be added to the creamed yeast fluid. The stamens, which are from the saffron crocus (*Crocus sativus*), can also be added the mixture. Cover the bowl with a damp cloth and place in a warm place to prove. This process takes about 2–3 hours. After the mixture has been proved place it into prepared baking tins and cook in the centre of the awven at Gas mark 3 (330 F) for 1½ hours.

Saffron: more valuable than gowold...

Over the centuries, saffron has been so coveted that it has started wars, and pirates have valued it above gold! Yet it is easily grown, and rather than being an exotic crop it can actually be grown in Britain (Saffron Walden in Essex was a growing and trading centre). But it is a very labour intensive crop, hence its great cost. Saffron was prized by plague victims, who believed it had medicinal properties, yet plague wiped out the saffron growers and thus opened Mediterranean markets.

■ A dish of limpets, me 'ansome?

As a seafaring community it was the obvious choice of villagers to look to the beach and sea for food. Cockles were scraped from the mud flats at Skern; mussels were plucked from the mussel beds when they 'ebbed up' (were exposed by the ebbing tide) in the middle of the river; winkles were prolific on the rocks at west Appledore; and, of course, there were limpets.

All these molluscs were taken and eaten in season. Cockles and winkles were picked during the summer months and mussels were taken in the autumn, usually at the Spring tides, which occur in September, October or November. However, if there had been heavy rainfall and the river had been in spate the gatherers would wait a week or two until the river had drained out all the detritus and freshwater carried from field run-off to allow the shellfish to clean themselves with seawater. Mussels were the favourite mollusc to pickle in vinegar for consumption during the winter months, usually as a treat for 'Sunday tay'.

Before the refrigerator became a household must-have, Appledorians had a 'safe' – the Appledorian term for a cool larder – suspended in the back yard. These were substantially constructed using hard wood and metal gauze, with a hinged door or a pair of doors. The door or doors were kept closed by a wooden or brass button. This sturdy construction had a cool slate slab bottom and even, perhaps, a shelf or two with smaller pieces of slate on which food stuffs were placed to keep cool. The safe was usually hung on a north-facing wall in the back yard, well up off the ground so that the rats or mice could not easily find the stored food. If they did find a way into the safe then the rat gin or cage would be deployed to catch the offending rodent. Cooked and raw meat would be stored in the safe along with milk, cream, butter, lard and dripping.

Today people have a seafood platter containing cockles, mussels, winkles and other molluscs and crustaceans, but mention limpets and it appears that it is very rare that the limpets are used as a culinary delicacy. There are several species of limpet inhabiting the waters of the British Isles, but the one eaten by the Appledorians was the Common limpet (*Patella vulgata*). Only the smaller ones were harvested, as the larger, older limpets would have been very tough and rubbery. It is the muscular foot that enables the creature to move around its rocky environment, grazing with its file-like tongue on young, green seaweed fronds. Getting these creatures off their rocky home is difficult, but with a surprise quick blow they can be dislodged cleanly.

After being collected they were soaked in fresh water to clean them, then removed using a small knife to loosen the flesh from the shell. The entrails would be discarded and the foot washed and boiled for five minutes or so. After being drained the limpets were minced using a mincing machine clamped to the kitchen table. Breadcrumbs from thick-cut stale white bread was made by crumbling the slices with the

Mussels, limpets and winkles at Westward Ho!

hands, and a very large bundle of parsley from the garden was washed and chopped and mixed together with the limpets and salt and pepper. To cook, a knob of lard was put into a large iron frying pan and heated, and the mixture added. It was cooked slowly and turned over from time to time until the cook was satisfied it was done. Preparing and cooking limpets in this way ensured that they were not going to be tough and rubbery and they were, in fact, a good source of protein.

■ Laver: the edible seaweed

Laver (*Porphyra umbilicalis*), though technically not a plant but a type of algae, is picked from the pebbles and rocks in the inter-tidal zones along the coast from Westward Ho! to almost as far as Bude. It is at its best during the winter months when the weather is colder and a frost has been on it. Appledorians have always loved their laver. During the summer months when the water is warmer it is left to grow and if it has been a good season it can grow to six or eight inches in suitable sites.

In recent years, the accretion of sand on the pebble beds at the back of Northam Burrows and grazing by the large numbers of Brent geese (*Branta bernicla*) that now overwinter in the estuary, there is less and less of this favourite food to be found near Appledore. Laver pickers are therefore being forced to travel further afield to harvest it

Laver is found more commonly along the western coasts of Britain and Ireland, thus it became a popular food source among the Celtic races. In Wales it is known as laver bread, in Scotland as slaak, and in Ireland it is known as sloke.

Appledorians still enjoy their laver accompanied by thin slices of belly pork, known locally as 'henderland bacon', and 'heel taps' – cold boiled teddies (potatoes) sliced in a shape that resembled shoe heels and fried in the bacon fat. Sometimes raw teddies are used and when they are it is known as 'raw teddy fry', but the teddies are still called heel taps

Strong-growing laver on the pebble beds

because of the shape. If raw teddies are used, the teddy is sliced thinly and placed in the frying pan with some lard and an enamel plate placed over the top to steam-fry them. When they are softened the plate is removed and the teddies allowed to brown. The laver is warmed in the frying pan in which the bacon has been fried: usually the laver has already been prepared and cooked by the person who has gathered it and it is sold ready to eat. It can also be eaten cold, but most people enjoy the laver prepared as above.

■ *The two samphires...*

Plants of the seaside were also utilised as a food source not only by Appledorians but also by other coastal communities around the country where the local geology provided suitable habitats for these plants to grow – long before it became fashionable for upmarket restaurants to serve them! – and, of course, these plants were free. Some of these plants were gathered from the beach and from the pebble pavements behind the pebble ridge in the vicinity of Northam Burrows, now a Site of Special Scientific Interest (SSSI).

Marsh samphire (*Salicornia europaea*) was gathered from the mud flats of the Skern and has been a favourite food for generations. It was gathered from the muddy salt marshes of the estuary, usually in the late spring or early summer, while it was still young and succulent. After it had been washed and gently boiled it was served as a vegetable or was pickled and used to accompany cold meat.

Rock samphire (*Crithmum maritimum*), as the name suggests, prefer the habitat of rocky, pebbly shores or cliff faces that are often in the splash zone of the sea in other parts of the estuary. At Northam Burrows, rock samphire did not grow as prolifically as marsh samphire, but small amounts could be found on the pebble pavements between the large dune

The cactus-like stems of Marsh Samphire on the Skern

Rock Samphire clinging to the seashore rock face

systems of Greysands, though these have now largely disappeared. They still flourish, however, on coastal cliffs and stony areas near the sea all along the North Devon coast.

Rock samphire was collected and eaten raw as a salad vegetable or pickled in spiced vinegar and used as a relish with meat. Samphire and the earlier 'Sampere' or 'Sampier' is from the French Herbe de St. Pierre, the herb of the fisherman Saint whose name was Petros or Rock (St. Peter). It was thought that eating this plant prevented or alleviated symptoms of stones or other troubles with the kidneys or bladder.

■ Junket and craim

Finally, in this section on traditional Appledorian food there are two items I can always remember my Gran Bennett and my mother making, both being a favourite as they were always served together, perhaps as a treat for 'Sunday tay'. First, junket: not much heard of these days as a sweet (but is still a favourite and still served at the pub in Parkham); and the making of clotted 'craim' (cream).

Junket is a dish that was often given to 'invalids' in an attempt to build them up. The ingredients are full craim milk – usually about a pint, some caster sugar, nutmeg and two or three teaspoons of rennet – an enzyme obtained from the stomach of cows that can usually be bought at health food shops.

Making junket is as easy as making a jelly. First, pour a pint of full fat milk into a saucepan, put on a *gentle* heat, add the sugar and stir until the sugar has dissolved. At this point dip a finger into the milk to ascertain the temperature: the milk should not be allowed to go any higher than body temperature because the rennet will be rendered useless by high temperatures. Add the rennet and stir; pour into serving dishes and grate some nutmeg over the top. Because the sweet is at body temperature it can be eaten as soon as it has set, which usually takes only a few minutes. Just before serving add a dollop of home-made clotted craim on top – 'ansome! I remember my Gran adding a medicinal tot of brandy to her junket to make it just that bit more special.

Most people made their own craim on the top of the Bodley on a cool area at the back of the stawve. All that was needed was an enamel bowl and a pint or two of full craim milk. This was poured into the bowl and stood on the cool part of the stove for several hours and left there overnight, the next morning the craim would be scooped off the top of the milk and put into the craim dish – all craimy underneath and crusty on top. The left-over milk would then be decanted into a jug and used by the family. Fresh milk delivered again that day would be treated in the same way, thus there was always a dish of craim on the table and it was very often used instead of butter. Indeed, a favourite Sunday tay time treat of 'thunder and lighting' consisted of a slice of bread with craim generously spread on it, and then some golden syrup drizzled over the top. They old Appledorians certainly knew how to live, even though there was very little money or home comforts to be had, making do and mending was the order of the day for them!

❖❖❖❖❖❖❖❖❖❖❖❖❖❖❖❖

Afterword...

Today it would not be safe for a cheel of ten to be left to their own devices in a 10-foot punt. The river traffic during the summer months is phenomenal: so many people these days have the ability and the resources to get on to the water. During the summer months visitors from up-country add to the locals from around the district and sweep into the village in huge four-wheel-drive vehicles and trailers loaded with craft up to 20 ft.long. Driving to Churchfields car park they pay their tenner, launch their boats into the river, open the throttles of the twin 90hp outboards, and head out to sea. At the mouth of the estuary there is the notorious Bideford Bar, something the locals respect, but these sailors seem not have any respect for it, and even for their own lives, so they certainly have no thought for others. The saving grace of this confluence of the rivers Taw and Torridge is the vast rise and fall of the tides, which has so far deterred the construction of a marina or two.

It is not only this little village tucked away on the edge of the Taw and Torridge estuary that has seen huge changes; other towns and villages have also undergone an almost complete metamorphosis. But it is the small, tightly-knit coastal communities like Appledore that have felt the greatest impact. What was once a community of friends and family where no one locked the door – day or night – has turned into a community of 'us and they'. The 'Sooners', as they were known when they first came to the village, was not a compliment. It was a case of 'the sooner they go, the better'! In the country areas we have Sooners complaining about the country smells: at one time, when someone complained to my mother about the dreadful smell of the manure that she was spreading on her garden, she just turned around pulled the bit of rag from her old brown coat wiped the dew-drop off her nose and said,

'Wull, me 'anse, there's plenty over the churchyard that would love to be able to smill that.' The lady went in and shut the door without a word! And recently there was a case where the sight and smell of dead fish on the quayside have been objected to by visitors who have walked along the fish quay at Ilfracombe!

The old skills are also disappearing. The knitting of Appledore frocks is fast becoming lost within the village as the maidens of our generation get older and the following generations do not have the interest and do not wish to learn the craft. The building of small boats from traditional larch and oak is also becoming obsolete because carbon fibre and GRP hulls are comparatively inexpensive, almost maintenance free and are built on a production line in a factory. Gone are the little boat-building sheds at the bottom of the courts in Irsha Street: these have now been converted into residences, and the entrances to the drangs which lead to these properties now have notices saying 'Private Property'. But as children we would run and play around these drangs as they all interconnected, having great fun playing cowboys and Indians. So even that innocent pastime is in decline. Making and mending of nets is another skill that's hardly seen today – the list could go on.

With this gradual decline of the traditional in my mind, in 2008 I started to think about the mat-making my father use to do, using old natural fibre rope that he found; usually sisal, hemp or manila. He would spend hours unlaying the rope and then even more hours plaiting it up again into sennit. But that was not the end of the process, the sennit was then sown into the traditional shapes and sizes of what is known as the Appledore mat.

Another type of mat my father made was the compass mat. This had previously been recorded as being called a 'bicycle wheel mat' because, it was said, without any real evidence, that the sailors used the rim of a bicycle wheel as a type of template – but where exactly the old salts

A typical Appledore rope mat

A compass mat made by Walter Ford

who went to sea on the sailing ships would get a bicycle wheel on ship was unrecorded. However, recently, through conversations with a family member who had been taught mat-making skills by my father, it emerged that this type of mat was always referred to as the compass mat. This was because the mat was made by initially having strands of rope coming away from the centre as north, south, east and west. Two more strands put into the centre were north-east, north-west, south-west and south-east. These were not laid over one another but arranged in a 'V' so that they were in the centre of the area between the north–south and the east–west strands. The strands were held together with a simple overhand knot using the north–south strand, which is a few inches longer than the other strands. As the mat was being made these strands were kept straight, and as the mat grew more strands were added – and kept straight, until the required size was achieved: at about the point when 64 strands had been incorporated: the number of points on the card of old compasses (today it is normal for a 32 card to be used). So there's still a lot to be learned from embracing the old skills and crafts!

It is unfortunate that today there appears to be little interest in these traditional crafts. Some who have taken to making Appledore rope mats have found the craft much too time-consuming and, as the natural fibre rope has to be purchased, the cost can be prohibitive. But the sailors who made them during the age of sail would have been at sea for many months and would have had a ready supply of old rope such as rigging and the like when it was replaced with new. So, to the sailor, mat-making became a pastime between watches; when on a long reach; or when the ship was weather-bound in port. It was not something that could be done in a week or so. If a mariner was away on a long voyage – sometimes for over a year – he would come home with perhaps two or three mats he had made, and they were always proudly displayed by his family on the front doorstep or in the porch for all to see. Similarly,

Appledore frocks are rarely knitted these days, as the price of these hand-knitted garments, which take many hours of work, is prohibitive. Plus the fact that traditional navy blue worsted wool is increasingly difficult to obtain.

It is sad, but it is probably not just in Appledore that these traditional crafts are being lost. I suspect that in other locations around the country other skills and crafts are disappearing just as fast.

The changes that have occurred in Appledore and other communities from just before the Second World War have been unbelievably life-changing. Today, if a man dies on a voyage with a friend – as in the case of Captain White – the news would travel the world in minutes, and a whole panoply of rescue services might be in attendance – although the survivor of the voyage would probably be arrested on a possible murder charge! Progress? I wonder.

It is not just the old traditional crafts we are losing – a village such as Appledore has always had a plethora of characters, both male and female, but as time goes by they too are lost, and the younger generations following along have not had to endure the experiences that a hard life produces. The old characters got on with life as they knew it and just considered that it was the same for everyone else, which in general it was, and in consequence they took life as it came and were able to laugh and joke about it afterwards. Many a yarn has grown out of such experiences and will probably live on for many years to come, passed down by word of mouth or in books like this one. The younger generations cannot be blamed for these changes, even the older generation has come to embrace the new technologies and are probably enjoying life now far more than they had ever done previously in their lives. But even so there are still a few of the old generation who remember the days of their childhoods and the life skills that were taught to them by their peers.

Many 'incomers' try to become Appledorians, but they very often fail, even if they can claim to have had fathers or mothers who went away from the village when they were young. But these 'emigrants' rarely came back to the village during their lifetimes and can hardly be called Appledorians. During the Second World War members of the armed forces came to the village and some met and married Appledore maidens, and these men integrated well into the village, but they never laid claim to being Appledorians: they knew that they had to be 'over the churchyard for at least 50 years' before they were even to be considered as one! And if they did claim to be an Appledorian the local men would soon put them in their place and they'd be told, 'You've only lived 'yer five minutes' – even if they had 'lived 'yer for 40 years'! 'You can put a man into Appledore but you cannot put Appledore into a man': a saying that is as true today as when it was first said many years ago when the village was discovered by the Sooners a few years after the Second World War…

❖❖❖❖❖❖❖❖❖❖❖❖❖❖❖❖❖